MOVABLE FEASTS

MOVABLE FEASTS

A Reconnaissance
of the Origins and Consequences of
FLUCTUATIONS IN MEAL-TIMES
with special attention to the introduction of
Luncheon and Afternoon Tea

by

ARNOLD PALMER

Oxford   New York
OXFORD UNIVERSITY PRESS
1984

Oxford University Press, Walton Street, Oxford OX2 6DP

London New York Toronto
Delhi Bombay Calcutta Madras Karachi
Kuala Lumpur Singapore Hong Kong Tokyo
Nairobi Dar es Salaam Cape Town
Melbourne Auckland
and associated companies in
Beirut Berlin Ibadan Mexico City Nicosia

First published 1952 by Oxford University Press

First issued as an Oxford University Press paperback 1984
with an introduction by David Pocock

British Library Cataloguing in Publication Data
Palmer, Arnold
Movable feasts.—(Oxford paperbacks)
1. Mealtimes—Great Britain—History
I. Title
394.1'2 GT2853.G7
ISBN 0-19-285141-1

Printed in Great Britain by
The Guernsey Press Co Ltd
Guernsey, Channel Islands

Or if in 'tittle-tattle, toothpick way,
Our rambling thoughts with easy freedom stray.

Churchill's *Night* (1761)

CONTENTS

ILLUSTRATIONS

INTRODUCTION

'SHALL you be at home tomorrow morning?' asked Lord
Orville; and, on Evelina's assurance that she was likely to
be found, he added, 'About three o'clock?' With this
quotation from Fanny Burney's *Evelina*, published in
1778, Arnold Palmer illustrates his description of meal-
times as 'the hinges of the day', meaning that it is not the
clock that tells us which part of the day we are in but rather
the meals that we eat. In the days when dinner was eaten
in what we would call the early afternoon it was morning
until one had dined, and this extension is not so odd when
we reflect on our own usage. We should think it odd if
someone greeted us with a 'Good afternoon' at 12.15
because for us the afternoon begins when we have had our
midday meal.

Arnold Palmer's investigation into the ways in which
meal-times changed, and the reasons why, is confined to
the vanished world of 'gentlefolk' for the good reason that
there was more evidence on their habits than on those of
the majority, and it was also a world that he knew, as is
clear from his description of himself as a guest in a large
comfortable house at the turn of the century: 'I remember
[a footman] who took out, ironed, and reinserted the laces
in my shoes.' The people with whom he was concerned
had finished their shopping by 3 o'clock and we must look
elsewhere, to Mayhew for example, to learn something of

INTRODUCTION

the people who worked through the day and night to
produce the silks, the leather, and the lace, those who
counted themselves lucky to have dinner at all (*The
Unknown Mayhew*, edited by E. P. Thompson and Eileen
Yeo, Pelican Classics, 1973).

The reader with retrospective social conscience may be
consoled to learn that the elegant assemblies of gentlefolk
were occasionally noisome affairs. In the nineteenth
century the London houses of the rich were the first to be
connected to sewers in a rather primitive manner, and we
know of one 'gentleman of distinction' who suffered on
this account most particularly when he was entertaining
his friends: 'whenever he had a party there was a stronger
fire in the kitchen, and stronger fires in other parts of the
house, and the windows and external doors being shut,
and a greater draught created, larger quantities of the foul
air from the sewers rose up' (J. L. and Barbara
Hammond, *The Bleak Age* (Pelican edition, 1947), p. 62).
But it would be foolish to criticize Palmer for not writing a
different sort of book and he will not be found either
complacent or lacking in compassion; he was, moreover,
very conscious of the complexities of his subject even
within the confines of that section of society which he
chose to study. As he says in his Introductory: 'Hardly
anything in this book is quite, quite true, or would not be
the better for qualification', and 'Who can say, today, at
what hour the Englishman breakfasts? It depends on
which Englishman one has in mind.'

Let us look, for example, at an author who was (I
estimate) a near contemporary of Palmer—D. H. Law-

rence, whose novels Palmer does not call in evidence.
From *Sons and Lovers*, first published in 1913, we can see
how much more complicated Palmer's task would have
been had he attempted a more comprehensive work and
considered evidence which he was less well placed to
interpret. There he would have found that among the
mining families of Nottinghamshire in the last decades of
the nineteenth century mothers and children ate their
dinner at an hour which Oliver Cromwell would have
recognized: 'William appeared at half-past twelve . . .
"Can I have my dinner mother?" he cried, rushing in with
his cap on . . . "You can have your dinner as soon as it's
done," replied the mother . . . "it will be done in five
minutes. It's only half-past twelve." ' On that occasion
they ate batter pudding and jam. Later we learn that Mrs.
Morel had always two dinners to cook: 'she believed that
children should have their chief meal at midday, whereas
Morel needed his at five o'clock. So Mr. Heaton would
hold the baby, whilst Mrs. Morel beat up a batter pudding
or peeled the potatoes.' But in the farming Leiver family
where Paul Morel had his dinner on the day that Miriam
burnt the potatoes, the men of the family had their dinner
at midday. When Paul Morel began to earn however, he
encountered eating habits that Arnold Palmer would have
recognized. 'He went out to dinner several times in his
evening suit' and told his mother of 'these new friends who
had dinner at seven-thirty in the evening'.

Palmer's task would have been made more difficult still
had he tried to trace the history of 'tea' (not afternoon tea)
as a meal outside the world of gentlefolk. From

INTRODUCTION

Lawrence's novels it would seem that at least in the late nineteenth century it was limited among the mining communities to Sunday afternoon, following, I presume, a Sunday dinner at midday. At the same period, however, as witness Mr. Pooter and *The Diary of a Nobody*, there was such a thing as 'meat tea' at the end of the working day, distinct from supper which was later. How and when did 'tea' come to be the name for the main meal at the end of the working day? We might have thought industrial workers would have followed the pattern of D. H. Lawrence's Mr. Morel and simply moved their 'dinner' on from midday to evening, so emulating the practice of the more leisured; but clearly this did not happen. It may be that 'Afternoon Tea' served at 5 o'clock in polite society provided the model first for office-workers and then for manual workers, although as regards *substance* the genteel collation of the drawing-room seems an inadequate name for a proper meal; moreover this line of argument does not explain why the word 'tea' should replace the socially approved word 'dinner'. Connected with all this is the emergence of the term 'high tea' which suggests that whoever invented it wanted to distinguish between the more substantial evening meal and 'low' (presumably afternoon) tea; but afternoon tea was not a regular working-class meal.

The elevation of the word 'tea' to describe the main meal must have been a rapid process. In the 1840s tea was still not a common drink. 'Congou, the quality usually drunk by the working classes, cost . . . 3s. 4d. [a pound] with duty: it is not surprising that at this period consumption was only $1\frac{1}{2}$ lb. per head per year'. Cuts in the duty on tea, the development of the Indian tea plantations, and 'a fierce price-war' all combined to bring the price down, and in 1889 Liptons were able to offer 'The Finest Tea in the World' at 1s. 7d. a pound. No doubt the activity of the Temperance Movement did much to popularize the *drinking* of tea, but neither this nor the reduction in cost explains how in so short a time 'tea' became the name for the evening meal; all we can say is that by the year 1900 the usage was firmly established.*

Dinner was the major social event of the day in Palmer's world—a meal which it would be dull to eat alone, a meal for entertainment—and its history and its destiny very much concerned him. As to its future he was doubtful; he would no doubt have been gratified to learn that thirty years after his book was published there survived somewhere in British society the need for such occasions and the people capable of maintaining them. In *The Times* for 19 March 1983, Brian Masters celebrates the eightieth birthday of one of the few remaining social hostesses in London 'entertaining on a scale and in a style which most people presume to have vanished long ago . . . The Hon. Dorothy Burns gives three dinner parties a week when at home in Mayfair.'

Palmer noted the movement of the time of dinner from

* On the history of the price of tea and working-class budgets at the end of the last century see John Burnett, *A History of the Cost of Living* (Penguin, 1979), pp. 212–14, 267–74, from which the words quoted in this paragraph were taken. On the effect of the Temperance Movement, see Brian Harrison, *Drink and the Victorians* (Faber and Faber, 1971), pp. 301–3. I am grateful to my colleague Eileen Yeo for this reference.

11 a.m. in the reign of Henry VII to 9 p.m. in 1953, 'the most advanced time yet recorded'. It could not, he thought, advance further; might it then begin to retrogress? 'While these pages were being written, I have seen a notice from a small restaurant announcing that dinner is obtainable at 5.30, and from another smarter establishment, offering a meal at 5.45. There were people in the first decade of the nineteenth century who would have regarded such hours as slightly bourgeois.' Today it would seem that throughout the United Kingdom for those who dine out the average advertised time for dinner is between 7 and 11 p.m., but there are more than a few restaurants in London alone which advertise 'dinner' at 5.30 or 6 p.m. (*Egon Ronay's Lucas Guide*, 1983).

But dining in a restaurant, even dinner as *the* meal of hospitality, are not part of the regular experience of the majority of the population. An introduction to a history of meal-times must include some account, however cursory, of the meals eaten in houses up and down the country. My evidence will be that provided by some of the hundreds of people who write loyally for Mass-Observation on a variety of topics, one of which has been meals and meal-times, and food from every conceivable point of view*. First however, before I report on this testimony, some general considerations.

Arnold Palmer could assume a concord, with very minor variations of time, name, and substance in the subject of his enquiry; one of his witnesses might not take

---

* I am grateful to Eric Gulliver, a member of the original Mass-Observation team, who made a digest of these reports.

lunch, for instance, but would know both at what time other people did and the kind and quantity of thing that they would be eating. The only meal in current British practice which has a semblance of this predictability is breakfast. But at any time between 11 a.m. and 2 p.m, there will be people eating what they call dinner, lunch, a snack, or a midday meal, which may consist of anything from a cup of tea and a biscuit to a two- or three-course meal. At the end of their day's work they may have tea, or dinner, or supper, and although for the majority this is indeed the most substantial meal, we could not predict its substance from its name—even if it is called 'dinner' it may well be served with tea to drink; and it may be called 'tea' but tea may not necessarily be drunk with it. 'Supper' can also describe a substantial snack in the early or mid-evening, or it can mean tea and biscuits taken 'last thing'.

There are other general trends which have affected more what is eaten than when it is eaten. Diet consciousness has become a social fact since the war. In Mrs. Valentine's *The Young Woman's Book*, published around 1933, one of her contributors could say firmly that a 'woman requires every day $2\frac{1}{2}$ ounces of flesh-forming food, and $7\frac{1}{2}$ ounces of heat-givers. A man requires 5 ounces of flesh-formers and 10 ounces of heat-giving materials.' Today there appears to be scarcely a household in which a concern with slimming or heart diseases has not altered or reduced the daily intake; steamed puddings, for example, have all but vanished although they are remembered with affection. Connected with this is the growth of vegetarianism and something of a decline in meat-eating. Men, more than women, tend to regard a meal without meat as no meal at all. Nevertheless in many households meat may only appear on the menu about three times in the week; for it is now regarded as an expensive item that can be replaced by convenience foods. It is also interesting to note that whereas in the 1930s a housewife might distinguish between home-made and bought, or 'shop', cake and jam, now we find the need to specify that a spaghetti bolognese or a curry is 'home-made'. In general the weekday meals are governed by the need to save time; and whereas the generation of those who are now parents looks back with self-denying regret to spotted dick, dumplings, and meals rich in flesh-formers and heat-givers, the adults of the future may sigh for fish-fingers, baked beans, frozen peas, pizza, and the ubiquitous quiche—in comparison with what in the first decades of the twenty-first century it does not do to imagine. But there may be hope in the fact that Sunday dinner, as we shall see, preserves its traditional form and honourable position.

Now for the meal-times in the 1980s. I shall use as my frame a book which Arnold Palmer must have known but does not cite, Mrs. J. E. Panton's *From Kitchen to Garret*, published around 1890, a manual of advice for a young middle-class couple, Edwin and Angelina, setting up house for the first time and able to afford no more than two maids.

The working week

Mrs. Panton strongly recommends an art pot with a plant

on it, a coco palm, and a few ferns in the centre of the breakfast table and around it 'three or four specimen glasses of flowers'. In front of Angelina is placed the breakfast equipage—coffee or cocoa, not 'that wretched tea that destroys so many digestions and unstrings so many nerves'; in front of Edwin the bacon, the curried eggs and rice, the kidneys; mushrooms are particularly recommended as 'a most healthy dish and not too expensive'. Today, despite Mrs. Panton's advice, tea is almost universally the favoured drink at breakfast during the working week, coffee often being reserved for the weekend.

Obviously the determining factor of the time of breakfast is the time that work starts. A shop assistant with no children in Southport, Lancashire, writes: 'My husband gets his own breakfast at 5.30—cereal, toast, tea. I have some muesli, toast and cheese, and tea at about 7.30.' The latest recorded time for breakfast is that of an all-night lorry driver whose breakfast is at 2 p.m.; for the other members of his family of five breakfast stretches from 6.30 a.m. for the eldest son to 9 a.m. for his wife after she has got the other two children to school. Overall, the average time is between 7 and 8 a.m. and, as so many people report, it is not a family meal in the sense that everyone sits down at the same time to eat the same thing. A typical account comes from Maidstone in Kent of a family in which both husband and wife work full time, and their two teenage sons are still at school: 'I can't eat breakfast, but I have two or three cups of tea. My husband usually has bacon and egg and the boys get themselves cereals—they all drink tea.'

INTRODUCTION

This report is representative on three counts. First, although cooked breakfasts during the working week are not common, when we do hear of them (and it may only be a matter of a boiled egg) they are cooked exclusively for men. This rarely indicates that the men will eat less later. Secondly, although there are men who have no more than a cup of tea or coffee at breakfast-time, this meagre basis for the morning's work is reported more frequently by women. Whether at home or at work these women may make up for the inadequacy by a mid-morning snack, but they are not likely to eat much—certainly no more than male office-workers are likely to eat at that time. Thirdly, cereals: the great majority of the reports on the working-day breakfast make up a litany of brand names from Alpen to Weetabix, and 'cereal', occasionally followed by toast, has become so much the main item of the British breakfast since the war that it may be thought surprising that it calls for any comment at all. Let us note two things about it, however: the manner of its serving and its use. First, to speak of 'serving' reflects middle-class usage before the war when it was indeed 'served' and appeared on the table in a bowl from which it was almost impossible to help oneself tidily with the tablespoon provided; this was a time when the origin of almost all 'bought' food was concealed, jams and marmalades were scooped into appropriate receptacles, and the jam or marmalade spoon was fitted with a little hook at the back so that it could, in theory, hang inside the pot. After breakfast the residue had to be scraped back into its original container and the pot was washed; I can remember the frowns which met a glass marmalade pot which appeared on the breakfast table just as it had left it the previous day. It is probably true to say that the cereal packet was the first commercial product to appear undisguised at the breakfast table. It was followed by the jam or marmalade jar, but the milk bottle which already stands unashamed on many breakfast tables has yet to be universally accepted. Breakfast, for obvious reasons, is the vulnerable point for all changes which make for speed and simplicity; how many butter knives survive in daily use? The second point to be noted about cereals is their utility as a 'convenience food'; they are no longer exclusively associated with breakfast—they are eaten at mid-morning by women at home, by children when they come back from school, and last thing at night when the evening meal has been early or (for whatever reason) missed. A correspondent in Basildon reports: 'So we always have a big packet of Kellogg's and then three or four of the more expensive brands to sprinkle on top.'

Breakfast at the weekend calls for special treatment later, and I now move on to midday and what Mrs. Panton describes as 'that most necessary of all meals— luncheon'. (I draw the reader's attention in passing (and *pace* Miss Nancy Mitford) to the ruling of Almack's Club in 1829, mentioned by Palmer, that for polished society 'lunch' was the term preferred to 'luncheon'.) Mrs. Panton continues, 'when little folks have to be thought of this midday dinner becomes a very easy business, but I must own that luncheon and the servants' dinner combined is a terrible trouble during the first year or two of married life'. She

warns Angelina of the dangers of having 'a tray brought up
with tea, bread and butter, and an egg', and points out
furthermore that the servants are less likely to grumble at
what has been provided for their dinner if it is the same as
their mistress's luncheon. Mrs. Panton's recommended
luncheon/dinners are based for the first part of the week on
the remains of a substantial roast of beef: '"dormers" can
be made with rice and cold beef, and sent in very hot, with
nice gravy' (is this some version of the Greek *dolma*?).
The meat course is followed by a pudding of sorts: 'a
mould of cornflower and jam is delicious'. Luncheon,
incidentally, was 'sent up' not 'served', and this, in
addition to the number of courses, distinguished it from
dinner. I find this distinction surviving in the 1930s: Mrs.
Valentine advises the Maid of all Work and Housemaid
that:

> By one, or half-past one o'clock, [she] ought to be dressed
> for the afternoon, and ready to bring in the luncheon or
> early dinner . . . She does not wait at table at luncheon; but
> leaving . . . all that may be required on the dumb waiter or
> waggon, goes to her own dinner. Though if it is an early
> dinner—not luncheon—the servants generally dine after
> the family.

In the 1980s the midday eating habits of many women
and men whether at home or at work would have caused
Mrs. Panton some anxiety. One of our correspondents in
South London collected details on three individuals:

> A is in her late twenties, married but supports a nine year
> old child from her first marriage by working part-time as an

office cleaner . . . in the morning she has a cup or two of tea and sometimes a slice of toast . . . She finishes work at about 1.30, usually does shopping and housework until about 3.30 when she collects her child from school. Other young mums join her for a cup of tea when they get home and they open up a packet of biscuits and sweets—usually something like a Yorkie or a Mars bar. This is the wife's lunch as far as I can see.

B is a young, single, working girl living at home with her parents. All that she would have in the course of a normal working day was 'cups of coffee and perhaps a Twix or Kitkat.'

C, a local government officer, aged about 55, has one cup of tea, one round of salad sandwich (made up by his wife), and an apple.

In general, working men and women take a 'packed lunch' (sometimes called dinner) to work, but if they buy food to eat at 'lunchtime' they tend to refer to it as a 'snack'. The change in this particular is noted by a business man now in his late forties who records details of the two-course lunches that he and other office-workers customarily ate in cheap restaurants in the 1950s; others noted the increasing number of people 'eating sandwiches, chips, and the like in London streets over the lunch hour'. It is in general true that the number of cafés and restaurants serving a set midday meal where working people eat regularly has decreased markedly over the last twenty-five years.

The name of the midday meal varies, as we have seen, although those who describe themselves as 'working class'

or 'of working-class family' stick with conscious deter-
mination to the term 'dinner' even if the meal consists of
sandwiches. We note that a house-decorator in Bristol, a
bricklayer in Leeds, and a motor mechanic in Sussex who
eat their 'dinners' at about noon open up what their wives
describe as 'packed lunches'. In general the word 'lunch'
seems to be winning as the meal to which it refers reverts
for the majority to something like its eighteenth-century
proportions (as Dr. Johnson described them, 'as much
food as one's hand can hold').

Outside the home the substantial pre-war lunch occurs
only occasionally for the majority, in the form of a
'business lunch' instead of the usual 'ploughman's'.* It is
found at home in two circumstances: first, when the
husband can return home at midday and there is a child
still at home; and second, among the retired. In Derby a
Gentlemen's Hairdresser can sit down, in the company of
his wife and son, to a lunch at 1 p.m. of steak or chops,
potatoes, and one other vegetable, followed by baked
pudding and custard, and a cup of tea. This is his main
meal of the day; in the early evening he will have
'something on toast' and in the late evening 'crackers and
cheese'. A retired couple in Leeds sit down together
between noon and 1 p.m. to 'a stew made from 1½ lb. of
beef shin, which lasts two days, dumplings added on the
second day—we are not pudding eaters, we get obese . . .
At Teatime (6 o'clock) we have a tomato sandwich

* Why 'ploughman's lunch'? The ploughman had to be at work as
early as 4 a.m. to attend to his horses. Consequently he needed a more
solid breakfast/lunch than other farm labourers.

(tomatoes are often too expensive, so onion, cheese, or jam replaces that)'. A retired secretary in Berkshire, living on her own, reports: 'I always have a joint on Sundays . . . this lasts me for four main meals with chips, salads, etc. . . . As I am not working it is toast and marmalade for breakfast and main meal at 12.30. Then a light tea of an egg or grilled cheese, no supper . . .'.

The great majority of women who are alone at home or looking after a very small child appear to eat remarkably little at lunchtime and few have more than 'the tea, bread and butter, and an egg' that Mrs. Panton deplored. Tea and biscuits, a bit of cheese, sometimes soup, sometimes cereals—these are the ingredients in most reports. Men and women out at work fare rather better but not by much; the standard appears to be sandwiches or rolls, and coffee—although for some there is shepherd's pie and beans at a pub. Unfortunately we do not have any reports on canteen food. But lunch remains a *time* distinct from any meal that may be eaten, as can be seen from 'I had a snack at lunchtime', or 'I worked over lunch' meaning that no lunch was eaten at all. To this extent lunch remains one of what Palmer called the 'hinges of the day' separating morning and afternoon. Our evidence for the remaining meals suggests that it may be fast becoming the only hinge.

Afternoon tea, to which Palmer devotes a whole chapter, seems, as an institution, to have vanished.* This

---

* It survives in hotels where it is now described as 'set tea', but the genuine article must be sought further afield, in British Columbia. There the Empress Hotel, Victoria, serves orange pekoe, sandwiches, *petit*

is not of course to say that the vast majority of our countrymen do not regard a cup of tea at about 4 o'clock as a necessity, but that the social occasion, the 'at home', preceded perhaps by a few hands of whist, has gone. If anything has replaced it, it must be the coffee-morning, a less august affair, organized for the sale of cosmetics or in aid of charity. Mrs. Panton highly recommended the 'delightful institution of five o'clock tea' and very sensibly observed:

> In a small house entertaining one's friends is too often a most arduous and tiresome business, because we will one and all of us attempt to do a great deal too much, and appear to be able to afford all kinds of luxuries that we cannot possibly manage, and I strongly advise any young bride with small means and a smaller *ménage* to confine herself entirely to afternoon teas.

Angelina is not to mind those who scoff at a middle-class woman 'aping her betters' and 'having her day at home'. The time between 4 and 5 o'clock, after one's drive or walk, could be a little depressing and was ideally suited to the regular meetings for tea and cakes. Such occasions survived through the thirties even in modest middle-class families who employed only a general housemaid. A man now in his mid-fifties recalls how at the age of five or six he improved the tea laid out in the drawing-room, before his

---

fours, buttered muffins, and crumpets, from 1 until 4.45 p.m. in Summer, and from 1.45 to 4.15 p.m. in winter. The management, to whom I am grateful for this information, call this 'Afternoon Tea' although it appears to be known popularly as 'high tea', which suggests a North American variation of native English usage.

mother and her guests came in, by providing each saucer
and tea plate with a doily carefully cut out from lavatory
paper.

Today 'tea' is for many the name of the meal at the end
of the working day, and given the exiguous amount of food
consumed by most since they got up in the morning it is
the main meal: indeed, often in our reports 'main meal' or
'evening meal' is the only name it has. This meal is also
still called 'dinner', and 'dinner' is both the meal served in
restaurants and the meal to which one may be invited in
the evening. However, a married professional woman in
Preston, Lancashire, writes: 'We are invited out to
"Supper" more frequently than to "Dinner". This saves at
least one course—preparation and cost.' She goes on to
note that 'it is now quite O.K. . . . to take a bottle of wine
with you when invited out'. In this connection I might
record the plea of a teacher in Sussex for some ruling on
etiquette here: 'I took a good bottle of claret and that was
the last I saw of it. What we had was rotten Spanish plonk
. . . A week later F thanked me and said he and J had
enjoyed our wine the previous evening!'

Dinner in the evening nowhere comes up to the eight
courses recommended by Mrs. Panton for inexpensive
little dinners for guests: hors-d'œuvres, soup, fish, entrée,
joint, game, sweets, savoury, or even the four or five
courses which Edwin and Angelina would eat when they
were alone in what Mrs. Panton describes as 'undoubtedly
hard times'. The nearest thing to it is reported from
Southport: 'Dinner, 6.30 or 7—grapefruit or soup,
chicken, liver, or other meat, potatoes or rice, vegetables,

then stewed fruit, ice-cream, or a pudding or melon.'
More typical is the report of a London cabby's wife,
mother of two sons still at school, who herself works as a
secretary:

> Dinner, *mostly* 7–8 p.m. (sometimes 8.30–9 if my husband
> is late but we don't always wait—depends!). Once a week
> *regular*, pasta—meat or cheese and tomato sauce; pizza—
> bacon/cheese/tomato topping; Fry Up—egg, bacon, ham-
> burgers, beans, sausages (mixture of two or three of these
> meats) plus beans or fried potatoes; steak and two veg. *or*
> steak and fried mushrooms, bacon, egg, etc.; fish poached
> in milk and two veg. About every *two weeks* little lamb
> chops and two veg. (boiled potatoes, peas or carrots);
> chicken and two veg. Very occasionally Kentucky Fried
> Chicken/Macdonalds/Chinese take-aways. We have fresh
> fruit for pudding in the summer, or tinned fruit and cream
> or carnation . . . In winter I tend to make more
> puds—bread and butter, macaroni, and something plus
> custard during the weekdays.

And typical of a childless working couple in their
mid-thirties is this from Bristol: 'Dinner: variable in the
extreme but always easy to prepare. If one or other of us
has had an easier/earlier day, they do the cooking—
omelettes, chops, frozen veg. Otherwise kebabs, curries,
Chinese take-aways (our stomachs are too old to cope
with fish and chips)'.

In case it might be thought that people will generally
call their evening meal 'dinner' if it is at 7 p.m. or later, let
us note that the earliest time recorded is 5 o'clock by a man
in Pembrokeshire, a retired clerk, now in his eighties; and

dinner' is at about 6 o'clock in many households, although
a telephonist in Norwich writes: 'The evening meal we
call dinner or tea, usually at about 6', and a mother of six in
Angus goes one better with 'supper-tea-dinner' to describe
her evening meal. Again, supper is not necessarily a late
evening meal. As we have seen, people are invited out to
'supper'. Our teacher in Sussex records: 'When I moved
down to London in the 60s it was always the old people
who had "dinner". We used to be invited out to
supper—anytime between 8 and 11 p.m.' In general,
however, the word 'supper' occurs much less frequently
than 'tea', 'dinner', or 'evening meal' and is not even
commonly used to describe the small or large snack—tea
and biscuits, sandwiches, piece of cake, bowl of cereal,
etc.—which in many households follows, at 9 or 9.30
p.m., an early evening meal. At the weekend and
particularly on Sunday, supper is restored when it has
been preceded by 'a traditional Sunday dinner' at about
midday. This is a return to the middle-class pattern of
the late nineteenth century; Edwin and Angelina would
only dine at midday on Sundays; their cold supper
on Sunday evening would permit the maids to go to
church.*

Where there are schoolchildren in the house their

---

* There is room for investigation. In *The Pursuit of Love* Nancy
Mitford describes the lugubrious lighting at the table when the Radletts
were joined for the first time by Captain Warbeck (Uncle Davey) for
dinner. However, when later in the meal Linda refers to one of the topics
unsuitable for conversation at table (the other two being religion and
politics), she is rebuked by Aunt Sadie: 'Get on with your supper and
don't talk so much.' (Penguin edition, 1951, pp. 28, 30.)

return sets off a round of food preparation which graduates into the evening meal. From Surrey:

> My little girl often brings friends home to tea—they eat at 5 p.m. as usually they are collected at 6. I make the children's favourites, fish fingers, sausages, hamburgers with chips, baked beans, similar 'Rubbish Foods', and usually they have ice-cream—jelly does not seem to be popular these days. My husband and I eat about 6 p.m.

In a family in Kent one son, having had a cafeteria lunch at school, returns at 5 to cereals, sandwiches, and cake; a little later a working son returns for a cooked two-course meal which is his tea; and our correspondent, together with her husband and youngest son who have had a substantial lunch, sit down to their tea of salad, or 'something on toast', and cake at about 6.15. We have very few reports of parents following what seems to be an older pattern in which they have a separately cooked meal after the children are in bed.

Sunday

In 1850 Mayhew recorded the following from a maker of cloth-button boots in the East End of London:

> it was a great struggle to get a crust for six of us . . . We were too poor . . . It was common for us to have breakfast about twelve, and dinner, tea, and supper last thing at night . . . I was obliged to work from five or six in the morning till twelve at night . . . we could, by long hours, get bread and coffee—meat we could not get. I could not get Sunday's dinner. We felt much hurt when the children told other

children that they had no dinner . . . We would reserve 2*d*. on Saturday night to buy pudding for them on Sunday; we thought that if they told their playmates they had pudding for dinner that would do. They, with ourselves, are now so used to do without, that Sunday's dinner, and other little comforts connected with a working man's Sunday, are looked upon as things that were. (*Unknown Mayhew*, pp. 313–14)

The strength of the traditional Sunday dinner stands out as one of the few stable facts in all the reports that we have received. Although beef is spoken of by many 'as one of the things that were', something to be bought only when guests are expected, there remains a good number of households where beef is still the required meat for the Sunday roast, and many more where it is preferred to the lamb, pork, or chicken which are the accepted substitutes when economy dictates. Yorkshire pudding, too, seems to be a necessary ingredient of Sunday dinner; in fact, even when beef has been reluctantly dropped it still often accompanies roast lamb or pork. Interestingly, the old practice of eating Yorkshire pudding with treacle or gravy before the meat and vegetables still survives in some households up and down the country. In most households the Sunday dinner, like the main meal on a weekday, is only a two-course meal and the second course, variously described as 'pudding', 'dessert', or 'sweet', is relatively light— a rice or sponge pudding is the heaviest that I have noted, and that usually in the winter; in the summer the second course is generally stewed or tinned fruit with custard, cream, or ice-cream. Let us notice also how frequently wine, whether bought or home-made, is mentioned as a regular feature of this Sunday meal by people whose parents never took alcohol with meals and drank wine only on very special occasions.

The time of this meal varies: between 1 and 2 p.m. seems to be the most popular time but a significant number of people prefer 7 or 7.30 p.m., and both times make for the restoration of traditions that appear to have vanished from the working week. A late dinner on Sunday favours the return, between 8 and 9 a.m., of what is known as the English Breakfast—bacon and eggs, fried bread, sausages, tomatoes, mushrooms. The earlier dinner encourages the return of high tea, a name which does not occur in a single report of weekday meals, and indeed only occasionally in our reports on the weekend; I have already noted the return of 'supper' as a light meal in the early evening when Sunday dinner has been taken at about midday. But Sunday dinner can float according to the other activities of the day and it would be absurd to suggest that it is *either* in the early afternoon *or* in the evening. A family of five in South london recorded the times of their Sunday dinners from May to August in 1982: they dined at home at 1.30, 3.00, 4, 5, or 6 p.m., and as the guests of relations at 1, 4, and 5 p.m.

If, however all these reports hint at the possibility of a change, it is that Sunday could give way to Saturday as the day of the weekly feast, and there are three reasons for this. First, the Sunday 'lie-in' which in several households has created the institution of a breakfast-lunch (described in only two reports as 'brunch'); secondly, a growing sense that the work and time required in the preparation and consumption of a large meal in the middle of the day could be better spent on other activities; and thirdly, Monday morning casts its shadow over Sunday evening. Our correspondents were asked to describe only their typical meals on weekdays and their main meal at the weekend (without further specification) and more than a few reported that if their Sunday meals were slightly different, they did not vary significantly from those during the week; but they added that if they had a special meal at all, and as often as not this was coupled with the indication that guests were invited, it would be on Saturday evening.

Mussolini, I am told, used to epitomize his view of the British as a luxurious and effete nation in the phrase 'a five meals a day people'. Arnold Palmer wondered whether the shape of the day as provided by set meal-times was crumbling altogether, and suggested a possible future in which we might peck our way through the day from snack to snack according to our whim or opportunity. Mussolini's view was never true of the majority; Palmer's fears have not yet been realized. What seems to have happened is that the pattern of the late nineteenth century middle-class family has shrunk both in the number of meals and the quantity of food consumed, while at the same time it has been extended to a far wider range of our society; it seems safe to say that in the process the times of breakfast, midday, and evening meals have become fractionally earlier. With regard to the names apart from breakfast, 'lunch' seems to have the edge on 'dinner' but it does not follow that 'dinner' is replacing 'tea' at the end of the working day. 'Supper' shows up poorly in our reports and yet it seems perfectly suited to resolve the ambiguities of both 'tea' and 'dinner'. Is the word on its way out, and have the young of the 1960s now become 'old' and so reverted to the terminology of their parents? Mass-Observation would welcome reports of any sightings.*

One aspect of meal-times which Arnold Palmer did not discuss and which can now only be touched upon in conclusion is their social quality within the family. Even in 1953 the refrigerator was not to be found in every house and the domestic freezer not at all, let alone the frozen foods and meals that go in it, and the only available 'take-away' was fish and chips. The fact that few people today are absolutely obliged to cook has meant that many, now free of the chore, are happy to practise the art. Similarly the fact that today anyone can feed himself from tin, packet, or foil could give heightened anticipation and pleasure to that communal 'main meal' at the weekend, whenever it is taken and whatever it is called. It would be too pessimistic to suppose otherwise, but in this, as in all that has to do with eating, people must decide for themselves what is good for them.

DAVID POCOCK

* Mass-Observation was founded in 1937 to record, for the purposes of historical research, the day-to-day lives of ordinary people. It does not operate with questionnaires, statistics, and samples but depends upon the willingness of volunteers up and down the country to write in their own way once a quarter on suggested topics. Anyone interested in joining Mass-Observation should write to the Director, Mass-Observation Archive, The Library, University of Sussex, Brighton BN1 9QL.

MOVABLE FEASTS

CONTENTS

I. Introductory

AMONG the innumerable domestic casualties of recent years an unnoticed stillness in the air, a modest gap in the hall, commemorate negatively the once vibrant gong. It used to summon us to meals, mysterious affairs prepared out of sight by unseen hands and popping up deliciously, in a setting of snow and silver, every four hours. It even bade us, in the more splendid mansions and hotels, prepare ourselves for the supreme evening rite. Beneath the master touch of one of those butlers whose glance, like Medusa's, one never dreamed of meeting, it could murmur, hum, and finally mount to a reverberating crescendo that made ears sing, temples throb, that drowned speech and thought and almost consciousness itself. It was the Victorians' monitory *apéritif*, the Edwardian version of the cocktail—and how, at its accents, those gastric juices flowed! Now that meals, like women, have lost their mystery, it is superfluous, it has gone. As father finishes laying the table, mother enters with the tureen, followed by the children with soup plates and toast-rack. Everybody knows that dinner is ready, knows it only too well and is already half-sick of the knowledge. As for evening clothes, they would only stress the fact that father has become a waiter and that mother has failed to become a cook. Who, then, wants a gong? Nobody. A generation has arisen which believes, rightly, that gongs have only one purpose—to usher in the films of J. Arthur Rank.

The gong was a relic of the days when meals were important and leisurely occasions—the days, that is to say, of every known century but our own. The pages of Mrs. Beeton, which we peruse today with mingled faintness and incredulity, would have aroused in our ancestors and the compilers of their cookery books—Plantagenet, Lancastrian, York, Tudor, Stuart, and Hanoverian—the response we give to brilliant, slight, rather decadent art. They would have regarded her, could they have scanned her work, as a Beardsley of the kitchen. Yet the change, which strikes us so forcibly, had long been in preparation. The war accelerated, extended, deepened it, but did not create it. The causes and results of this change—the effects of meal-times on our habits and of our habits on meal-times—are the subject of the following pages.

Much has been written of the kind of food and amount of food consumed by our forebears. Less has been heard of the times at which they congregated at table and of the way in which their meals fitted into the arrangement of their days. Here, it has seemed to me, is a corner of social history that could stand a little filling in.

For most readers the pleasantest history books are those

which are most precise. I share this preference; few people, if any, revere Macaulay more than I. Nevertheless, a small voice, refusing to be stilled, goes on endlessly whispering to me that history is far from being an exact science; that what appears to be true is, as a rule, only roughly true; and that if one can call two witnesses for every one called by the other side one has done exceptionally well. To readers who suffer increasing annoyance from my vagueness, I can only reply that, had space permitted, I should have been much vaguer and insisted on their company as I picked my painful way over rocks and holes to which, in my mercy, I here seldom allude. Hardly anything in this book is quite, quite true, or would not be the better for qualification.

Who can say, today, at what hour the Englishman breakfasts? It depends on which Englishman one has in mind.

In the main I have confined my attention to gentlefolk, for the reason that there is more evidence about them than about the rest of the population; and I have often, perhaps usually, looked for this evidence in novels rather than in journals and letters. If a diarist mentions the hour at which he dined, it is probable (whether he provides an explanation or not) that it marks a variation from habit. No novelist can afford to be so casual. If his characters eat at strange times, he must advance reasons to satisfy the reader. If he gives the hour without comment or without the invention of some deranging incident, we may assume that that is the hour customary at the time and in the circles with which he is dealing. His details, again, may be supported by the details in other contemporary novels; and when that happens we may, indeed, feel at last that we are approaching something like truth, that we are near to attaining the precision and enviable confidence that mark the most admired historians. And so it might be, were it not that, murmuring 'But yet I'll make assurance doubly sure', we consult just one more of those contemporary chronicles. . . .

In the course of the last few lines the word 'contemporary' has made two appearances, and perhaps should be submitted to even more emphasis. A great many novelists—I have been surprised by their number—tell stories laid in the not very immediate past. *Pendennis* and *Sylvia's Lovers* are but two names out of dozens and scores that might be mentioned. Mrs. Gaskell is possibly, Thackeray is probably, trustworthy; many of the sources on which I have relied were available to them, they had many sources of information not available to me. Nevertheless, with some hesitation and more regret I have ignored such novels as these. One cannot be sure of them. Events of which we have been witnesses, or of which we know the full history, are seldom accurately described in accounts reconstructed by the steadiest and most patient reporters. The lesson is chalked up every day; it does not seem difficult, but we die with it still unlearned.

Variations in habits are rarely abrupt. They are hardly visible unless specimens from rather widely separated periods are compared; but they mean something and, as soon as discernible, are worth studying, even the slightest of them. The sudden alterations in our hours of eating which occurred in 1940 are illuminating and exceptional because everybody knew then, and knows now, why they happened and what they meant. But the more gentle and distant rearrangements of the day had their causes, too. Hardly anyone except De Quincey has looked into their social significance, they tend to be forgotten. I thought it might be interesting to rescue, tabulate, and examine a few of them.

II. Seventeen-Eighty

A START has to be somewhere. For a number of reasons, which the reader may or may not deem sufficient, I choose the year 1780. The eighteenth century, which opened with a Stuart on the throne, had reached a point when it began, with rapidity, to acquire an almost modern aspect, when it seemed, one might say, to be preparing to retire in favour of the nineteenth. In many ways, of course, it was still its sturdy self. Johnson was there, and Reynolds; the Young Pretender had several years to live; the King was, if anything, too hale and hearty. But Chatham, Gainsborough, and Garrick had gone, Wordsworth, Constable, and Turner had come into existence. If the younger Pitt was still a law student, a new ensign named Arthur Wesley had been gazetted to the 73rd, a Highland regiment. Queen Victoria's Uncle George was already eighteen years of age, and a handful.

There were other inducements to think that the eighth and ninth decades of the century saw the birth of a new, and not yet dead, world. That far from clear-cut movement, the Industrial Revolution, was by all reckonings under way; a social upheaval of immense energy was in preparation on the other side of the narrow Channel. During the very long, exhausting, and precarious war or series of wars soon to upset the frontiers and equilibrium of Europe and ultimately to place England in a position never before attained and not yet wholly lost, the escape of the American colonies, now cutting themselves free, must have seemed remote and of only secondary importance. The young English of that day, the men and women born in or near the year 1760, were destined to be, for nearly forty years, sick to death of crises. For this reason alone we are nearer to them than any of the intervening generations.

One more reason remains to be mentioned. Beside the great events which produced the modern world it must appear pathetically, ludicrously trivial; but for my purpose it had great weight. There had recently been published, there was still being devoured, an anonymous novel entitled *Evelina*. After being attributed to Horace Walpole and other authors of note, it proved to be the work of a Miss Burney, twenty-six years old and the third child of an organist and musical historian. Within a few years the country was swarming with women novelists. Even of those who then achieved recognition, only two or three are now remembered; but a new tradition had been founded, and a lasting one. Miss Burney and her successors, especially Miss Edgeworth and Miss Austen, brought to the novel a domestic atmosphere, quietly realistic, different from, more pronounced than that which bathed even the interior scenes of Fielding or Smollett or Richardson. Others have appreciated the literary worth of these ladies. I praise them here for making my task easier.

The English of 1780 did not, of course, invent their day; they inherited it, made their modifications, and passed it on, as is done by every generation. They took over, with the rest, a steady tendency which had persisted throughout the century and throughout the centuries, a tendency for dinner, the main meal of the day, to become later. They may well have been unaware of it, for the tendency, having been very active during the reigns of the first two Georges, was in a lull. But its progress, if irregular, was irresistible, or seemed to be. A crisis—rebellion, revolution, war—usually gave it a little extra push, but even in peaceful times it had its own gentle impetus. At the beginning of the sixteenth century, Henry VII's England dined at 11 a.m. One hundred and fifty years later, Cromwell's England dined at 1 o'clock. By the beginning of the eighteenth century the hour was 2, and still moving on. Steele, though he was only fifty-seven when he died in 1729, noted that 'in my memory, the dinner hour has crept from 12 o'clock to 3'.

Familiar and convenient in warmer countries farther south, a long break in the middle of the day is ill-suited to our cooler, darker atmosphere. Nobody, however, seems to have been troubled by the waste of the daylight hours, the snapping of all continuity, the paralysis of the broken-backed day. On the contrary, the changes were invariably resented by the more responsible citizens, who saw in them nothing but manifestations of restlessness and instability by their immature and thoughtless juniors. A few years before his death Pope's friend, Lady Suffolk, was dining as late as four; and the poet, now turned fifty, came to the reluctant decision that he could not go the pace and must absent himself henceforward from her table at Marble Hill.

That was 1740, that was smart and highbrow Twickenham. To University Common Rooms and Cathedral

Closes Pope, with his habit of dining at 2, must have seemed no less skittish than the Countess. John Richard Green tells us that when, in 1723, Queen Caroline sent a buck to Magdalen, 'the dinner at which it appears is at 10 a.m. Each advance was made amidst grumblings from the older and more conservative members'. He goes on to quote from Hearne's diary of the same year:

> 'Tis an old custom for the scholars of all houses on Shrove Tuesday to dine at 10 o'clock, at which time the little bell, called pancake-bell, rings at St. Maries, and to sup at 4 p.m., which was always followed in St. Edmund's Hall as long as I have been in Oxford till yesterday, when they went to dinner at twelve and supper at six. Nor were there any fritters at dinner as there used always to be. When laudable old customs alter 'tis a sign learning dwindles.

Things moved, then, even at the Universities, and by 1767 Balliol had fixed the hour of dinner at 2 and of supper at 8. But the fashionable world kept its lead; by 1780 only the oldest inhabitants could remember Lady Suffolk's victory, only the most learned could be unaware of its consequences. The reader, on the other hand, if he pursues his way, will find his thoughts often returning to her, and to Pope. Behind and between all the pages of this book there is always a dashing hostess, there is always an ageing and discomposed celebrity. They are with us still; the struggle is constantly renewed, and no less regularly the lady wins. Perhaps it is as well that she should. But in the days just past, when Miss Burney had been scribbling away in secret at her *Evelina, or The History of a Young Lady's Entrance into the World*, she was clearly untroubled by the thought that that

9

World had known any innovations up to a day some eighteen months before her narrative opens. It is precisely this unconcern that keeps her story perennially fresh.

So here, now, and at last, with ties straightened and throats well cleared, let us turn to the day as revealed not only in the Burney novels and diary but in the diaries and correspondence of her contemporaries also. There is plenty of confirmation.

Breakfast

Since the stomach, the English stomach, does not care to remain inactive for more than four or five hours, breakfast advanced with dinner, though more slowly. In 1780, both in and out of London, it was and for some while had been customary to defer the first meal of the day till 10 o'clock. Most people had by then been up for two or three hours, but there was, of course, no hard and fast rule. Country-dwellers probably rose earlier than town-dwellers—the heroine of *Cecilia*, after her first night in London, 'arose with the light' and found herself amid sleepy servants doing the fires. Whether or not Miss Burney intended it, such behaviour certainly suggests a dewy innocence. But in both town and country much was accomplished during the hours before breakfast. Letters were written, housekeepers interviewed, walks taken, flowers picked and arranged, music practised and studies pursued, and calls, business or social, could be paid. When, for instance, a playwright arrived at Mrs. Thrale's before breakfast with a play in his pocket, the ladies were more flattered than amused or surprised. During the meal itself, visitors would often drop in and set themselves at table; such calls could be formal or informal, and their correct interpretation sometimes needed address. A few mornings after her defeat by the servants Cecilia, still the guest of the Harrels in their London house, found a Miss Larolles at breakfast. She did not learn till later that Miss Larolles had been 'waiting on her' and was gravely offended when Cecilia failed to pay a return visit within the regulation three days.

Breakfast was a highly conversational meal and it could go on for a long time—there is a breakfast in *Evelina* which lasts till nearly 1 o'clock—but usually it ended about 11. Nevertheless, it seems to have been still a fairly light meal, not to be compared with some of the breakfasts to be described in the following chapters. We read of a gentleman plying a lady with 'cakes, chocolate, or whatever the table afforded'. A Swiss pastor, C. P. Moritz, who spent a long and cheap holiday in England in 1782, was given no more than tea and bread and butter for his breakfast. 'The slices of bread and butter which they give you with your tea are thin as poppy leaves. But there is another kind of bread and butter usually eaten with tea, which is toasted by the fire and is incomparably good. This is called toast.' With breakfast at 10, elevenses were presumably not yet invented; but Moritz makes it clear that twelveses, oneses, or twoses were already a national habit. He noticed another national habit. 'I would always', he wrote, 'advise those who wish to drink coffee in England to mention beforehand how many cups are to be made with half an ounce, or else the people will probably bring them a prodigious quantity of brown fluid.'

Some years before he could buy a cup of tea, the Englishman could buy a cup of coffee; indeed, from the days of Charles II to the days of George II, more coffee was bought and brewed by the Londoner than by any citizen in the world. There is no evidence to show that he ever learned or wished to learn the knack of making it, or knew that there was one. Repeated efforts to instruct him have left him almost unmoved, and the time is approaching when we should, perhaps, acknowledge that he, like Lady Suffolk, has won.

Dinner

Dinner could be at any time between 3 and 5; by it, and not by the sun, the day was divided. A man or woman, if at home, would wear a house-gown and undressed hair until 2 or 3 o'clock. This was especially true of the City, where there were fewer idlers and less thought for appearances than in St. James's. It was 'morning' till one dined. 'Shall you be at home to-morrow morning?' asked Lord Orville; and, on Evelina's assurance that she was likely to be found, he added, 'About three o'clock?'

Our Swiss pastor, having few friends, dined at a coffee-house; he had no difficulty in finding one to suit him, a quiet, decorous place where clients read the newspapers and never dreamed of talking. There were coffee-houses for all tastes and purses, except those of the poorest classes. For them there were cook-houses, differentiated from the coffee-houses not only by their prices but also by their dirt and stench. Moritz, though he found a decent place, could not afford the better establishments, and resigned himself to 'a piece of half boiled or half roasted meat; and a few cabbage-leaves, boiled in plain water; on which they pour a sauce made of flour and butter, the usual method of dressing vegetables in England'. But at least he could satisfy his intellectual appetite. In the higher-class houses, where gentlemen would not dine under a guinea, quarterlies and magazines were provided and newspapers were filed for a year; for the tradesman spending 2s. at the chop-house, newspapers were as customary as salt-cellars; and even the mechanic, carrying his half-pound of beef or ham to the ale house, found newspapers there for those who could read. Authority, regarding the coffee-houses with an inflamed eye, mistook them for the cause, when they were merely the occasion, of the arguments of the disaffected. Under the Press restrictions of Charles II they were forbidden to sell reading matter; the managements, by providing it free of charge, added to the number and eloquence of their clients.

Four o'clock was the commonest hour. The Thrales at Streatham, Cowper and Mrs. Unwin in their retired Buckinghamshire village, and (for the most part) the hostesses of *Evelina*, all dined at 4. At about 3 o'clock reception rooms and gardens began to empty; for the costumes and *coiffures* of the age an hour was none too long. Lord Orville, then, timed his call at 3 o'clock with the express purpose of catching Evelina alone, and she was not for a moment deceived.

Keeping to the near side of 4 o'clock there were, as there always are, ancient bodies, like colleges and livery companies; and they were regarded then, as today, as picturesque at a distance but inconvenient at close quarters. In October 1786 Sir Joshua Reynolds scribbled a note to Boswell, offering to take him to dine with the Painter Stainers 'in their Hall in the City . . . as you love to see life in all its modes, if you have a mind to go I will call on you about two o'clock, the black-guards dine at half an hour after'.

Similarly, there were the spiritual, or social, descendants of Lady Suffolk whose efforts, though often premature and unsuccessful, were continual and, in the end, prevailing. A number of years had still to elapse before ordinary people, on ordinary occasions, dined later than 4; but, century after century, always kept up and always in the same direction, the pressure on the dinner-hour goes on. This pressure, sometimes weaker, sometimes stronger, never entirely relaxes even when the unpredictable day arrives and the garrison gives way. Individuals may hold out, social up-heavals may prove momentarily stronger; but the pressure goes on and, in the end, dinner is eaten a little later.

At the time with which we are dealing an invitation to dinner could be, in effect, an invitation to spend seven or eight hours in company, from 3.45 till 11 or midnight; and it covered more meals than one. Unallotted to one another in the reception room and unplaced at table, the party entered the dining-room in a polite mob, gentlemen bring-ing up the rear and at once manœuvring for position, and ladies, in spite of their recognized and practised helplessness, possibly finding themselves not too tiresomely surrounded. When the upstart Morrice seated himself next to Cecilia, Mr. Monckton by the use of a little ingenuity made him stand up for an instant, when he immediately inserted him-self into Morrice's chair. Except for Morrice's laugh there was no comment, not even of silence.

Ladies were for ever being handed in and out of coaches

and sedan chairs, up and down steps, in and out of seats at the theatre, through doors and past obstacles; but their hands, though sometimes kissed, were never shaken, and as we have seen they entered the dining-room without a supporting arm.

When the long meal was drawing to a close, the table-cloth was removed for dessert and wine. The ladies now usually, but not invariably, retired; if they went, one or more of the men might accompany them without exciting remark unless the party was smallish or the host touchy about his port; and if it was, as of course it was, the general custom of the ladies to depart for coffee and the men to remain for wine, we should note that, in a period now re-garded as highly formal, there was altogether greater free-dom than at a set dinner-party today. Any man with a weak head or an engaged heart might quit the circulating decanter and wander into the drawing-room whenever he felt like doing so. If he was quick, he might be in time for the coffee with which the ladies were presently served. 'Tea-board, urn and cake bearers' arrived about 8.30 and the gentlemen, warned by the butler, arrived with them, their legs presum-ably a little stiff after four hours and more at table.

In modest households, and when no company was enter-tained, the whole programme was naturally curtailed and the family ready for tea at any time from 7 o'clock, dinner having been at 4. (Today, in thousands of modest homes, where the last set meal is high tea at 6 or 6.30, tea with cakes and sandwiches is similarly welcomed some three hours later.) From the succulent pages of the Reverend James Woodforde we receive the impression that he sometimes drank tea and coffee simultaneously. He may well have done so after one of those simple dinners alone with his niece—'boiled chicken and a pig's face, a bullock's heart and a rich plumb pudding'.

Supper

Those cups of tea, those cakes and sandwiches fulfilled their little mission of revival. But even with their help a repast, however large, at 4 o'clock could not support people, least of all people of the eighteenth century, through the night and into the middle of the following morning. A further meal, varying in splendour with the establishment but commonly substantial, came on between 10 and 11— cold meats, sweets, fruit, and wine on ordinary occasions, a choice of hot dishes when company was present.

A hearty man like Mr. Woodforde, his natural appetite sharpened by Norfolk air, did not care to wait till 11, even when the presence of four or five friends gave him an excuse for a less frugal repast than the one just mentioned. There was that October night, when they sat down six at table:

> I gave them for dinner a dish of fine Tench which I had caught out of my brother's Pond in Pond Close this morning, Ham, and 3 Fowls boiled, a Plumb Pudding; a couple of Ducks roasted, a roasted neck of Pork, a Plumb Tart and an Apple Tart, Pears, Apples and Nutts after dinner; White Wine and red, Beer and Cyder. Coffee and Tea in the evening at six o'clock. Hashed Fowl and Duck and Eggs and Potatoes etc. for supper. We did not dine till four o'clock— nor supped till ten.

Woodforde's high colour catches the eye, but eighteenth-

16

century England was not exclusively rubicund. There were paler households, like Cowper's, where supper was 'a Roman meal . . . a radish and an egg'.

Theatrical performances began at 7. People going to the play would thus have no difficulty in dining and supping at home. If the rendezvous was at the theatre, or if a man and his wife went by themselves, dressing might be deferred till 6 o'clock, after dinner.

The day

In 1786, when she was fifteen years old, Lord Sheffield's daughter, Maria Josepha Holroyd, wrote a letter. She was at home, at her father's house in Sussex; she had not much news; and it may be doubted whether even she supposed that her letter—schoolgirlish, high spirited, shrill, and rather breathless—was of the faintest importance. But because she had the habit of telling her friends what they knew already, subsequent generations have noted and quoted her.

> I get up at 8, I walk from 9 to 10; we then breakfast; about 11, I play on the Harpsichord or I draw. 1, I translate, and, 2, walk out again, 3, I generally read, and, 4, we go to dine, after Dinner we play at Backgammon; we drink Tea at 7, and I work or play on the Piano till 10, when we have our little bit of Supper and, 11, we go to bed. . . . I think I have very near carried another point, which is to breakfast down stairs.

Precise and perfect, there is the story of one kind of day, and a far from uncommon one.

Evelina might doubt whether breakfast, compared with dinner and supper, 'may be called a *meal*', but its place in the

17

middle of the morning made it one of the two main hinges of
the day. Of this day there were three parts—before breakfast, between breakfast and dinner, and after dinner—and
for many months of the year the first and third divisions
were, as often as not, spent indoors.

Between the end of breakfast at 11 and the beginning of
dressing for dinner at 3, four hours were left for the day, or
for the daylight. They were uninterrupted hours, or could
be so for anyone prepared to forgo the 1 o'clock snack at the
pastry-cook's or the coffee-house; and for people of fashion,
with plenty of servants to do the household shopping, they
were apparently ample. But grumblings already were
audible about a domestic crisis, a difficulty of obtaining
servants or of paying their rising wages. In 1772 black
servants, who had hitherto been slaves and unpaid, became
free; some went home, while those who remained swelled
the wage-list. To us, today, the crisis does not seem very
severe; Mr. Woodforde, whose income was in the neigh-
bourhood of £400, could keep five servants at a total cost, in
wages, of £22. 10s. 6d. per annum. But everything is a
matter of comparison, and wages had risen and the once endless supply of likely girls and boys was increasingly and
noticeably being tapped by industry. The wives of men of
good income were, moreover, accustomed at this time to a
leisure which their mothers had not known. Admirable but
strenuous, the days had gone by when households were self-
supporting, when everything was made or provided at home.
Shops and itinerant tradesmen were rapidly increasing, and
the lady of fashion looked to her domestic staff to relieve
her of the routine work of catering and upkeep. She was,

therefore, very sensitive to even the shadow of a threat to the supply of labour, plentiful and cheap, and she easily grumbled. But, in fact, she was very far indeed from having much to grumble at, and we may leave her with her problem of filling in her four hours at a stretch, with no children to be taken to school, no queues to be joined, no one at home expecting a midday meal, no children to be fetched from school, no crockery and cutlery to be cleaned, no beds to be made, no absent charwoman to be wondered about. Perhaps I shall be expected to say that the pace, too, was slower, but anyone who has read *Evelina* and *Cecilia* must have his doubts on that point.

For the rest of the world four hours were not enough. We have seen that a certain amount of work, particularly correspondence, could be got through before breakfast; lawyers, politicians, civil servants (including the King and his ministers), the professional classes generally, all these often worked long hours after dinner. The equivalent of the modern business man, having an office in London and a house at Woking, hardly existed; his prototype seldom had or saw the need to work. Yet shops, including shops in fashionable districts, were open as long as twelve hours a day; and if, from the nature of their business, we are sometimes led to wonder what customers they served at 8 in the morning or 7 at night, it is clear that dinner at 4 was by no means a signal for the shutters.

For that considerable proportion of the public which had nothing to do, it would be truer to say that the hour was a beginning. The previous hours had been filled by visits to or from the tailor or dressmaker, in leisurely and talkative patronage of the bookseller, in attendance at rehearsal of a play or opera, in watching the conjuring up of Portland Place beneath the elegant wand of the Adam brothers, and everywhere and always in gossip—in brief, in collecting something smart to wear or talk about from 4 o'clock onwards.

In an age markedly social and sociable, the day was hardly long enough for all the little confabulations and for-gatherings so dear to the hearts of the models for Backbites and Sneerwells and Surfaces. The calls which began before breakfast went on until supper-time. Men-about-town of assured position, men like Horace Walpole, would wander out after dinner in search of ever more friends and ever more conversation. 'New-dressed by seven, went to Madame Walpole's, and then supped at Lady M. Churchill's', he noted, being then in his seventy-fourth year and rather proud of these 'feats of agility'. Invited or uninvited, he had no fear of being unwelcome; but other guests, especially if male and unattached, were frequently asked to come in for tea, cards, and supper, no slight being intended or felt by an invitation to join a party rising from the dining-table.

The dining club and the tavern are often indicated as promoters of still further sociability; but a French observer blamed them for 'the lack of society' which he found in London. In theory, and occasionally in practice, the *habitués* of such places passed the night in brilliant conversation. More often they were sunk, not an idea stirring, in the labours of digestion and the fumes of wine. Goldsmith, before ending up as a member of the most famous of all dining clubs, had experimented with other gatherings of

less illustrious company. From the boredom of those evenings he extracted nothing save matter for a good essay.

'The conduct of an Englishman's day in London', remarked that same Frenchman, 'leaves little time for work.'
Convenient enough for scions of the nobility, for moneyed
folk, heiresses and débutantes, possibly for artists and
writers, the day's divisions cannot have been anything but
awkward for men of affairs. Returning to their offices and
places of business at 5.30, after the long interruption of
dinner, they eventually got back home again at an advanced
stage of the evening, in time for tea if they were lucky or
else in time for supper and bed. They accepted their lot,
doubtless, like any other generation, unthinkingly or knowing no alternative or realizing that no rearrangement would
be workable if the rest of the world declined to join in.

For, however eye-opening the Grand Tours, whatever
the novel notions brought back excitedly from the Continent, everybody seems to have been following the same
sort of time-table. In her *Journal*, Madame la Marquise de la
Tour Du Pin gives a little picture of life in a big and busy
house in Paris just before the old France disappeared. It was
the winter of 1789–90; she was nineteen.

> I scarcely saw my husband except at breakfast, which we ate
> together, and at dinner. My father-in-law had ceased to give
> big dinners [on account of the revolution] but we always sat
> down twelve or fifteen at table, what with deputies or
> foreigners or persons of importance. Dinner was at four. An
> hour after dinner, spent in the drawing-room talking to
> various people who had dropped in for coffee, my father-in-
> law went back to his office. Unless I was going on some-
> where, I then returned home.

In England, the men seldom drank coffee in the drawing-room; it had gone by the time they arrived, they were the signal for tea. I have no evidence to suggest that the Marquise, at any hour, would have offered tea to the most masculine of guests. The increase, at once steady and rapid, in the popularity of tea was a phenomenon almost purely English, almost entirely eighteenth century. Tea will have, must have, a chapter to itself, but not yet.

Whatever the resemblance between the time-table of the English and the French, their table manners differed widely. François de la Rochefoucauld, paying visits to the Duke of Grafton at Euston and elsewhere, was in a perpetual state of surprise, from morning till night. In London he had been used to getting up when he chose, breakfasting (always with tea) at 10 or 11, and strolling about till he was ready for dinner. He found a régime at once more formal and strenuous, with the house-party taking

breakfast together, the meal resembling a dinner or supper in France. The commonest breakfast hour is 9 o'clock and by that time the ladies are fully dressed with their hair properly done for the day. Breakfast consists of tea and bread and butter in various forms. In the houses of the rich you have coffee, chocolate and so on. The morning newspapers are on the table and those who want to do so, read them during breakfast so that the conversation is not of a lively nature. At 10 o'clock or 10.30 each member of the party goes off on his own pursuit—hunting, fishing or walking. So the day passes till 4 o'clock, but at 4 o'clock precisely you must present yourself in the drawing-room with a great deal more ceremony than we are accustomed to in France. This sudden change of social manners is quite astonishing and I was deeply struck by it. In the morning you come down in riding boots and a shabby coat, you sit where you like, you behave exactly as if you were by yourself, no one takes any notice of you, and it is all extremely comfortable. But in the evening, unless you have just arrived, you must be well-washed and well-groomed. The standard of politeness is uncomfortably high—strangers go first into the dining-room and sit near the hostess and are served in seniority in accordance with a rigid etiquette. In fact for the first few days I was tempted to think that it was done for a joke.

Dinner is one of the most wearisome of English experiences, lasting, as it does, for four or five hours. The first two are spent in eating. . . . After the sweets you are given water in small bowls of very clear glass in order to rinse out your mouth—a custom which strikes me as extremely unfortunate.[1] The more fashionable folk do not rinse out their mouths but that seems to me even worse; for, if you use the water to wash your hands, it becomes dirty and quite disgusting. This ceremony over, the cloth is removed. . . . At this point all the servants disappear. The ladies drink a glass or two of wine and at the end of half an hour all go out together. It is then that the real enjoyment begins—there is not an Englishman who is not supremely happy at this particular moment. . . . This is the time that I like best; conversation is as free as it can be, everyone expresses his political opinions with as much frankness as he would employ upon personal subjects. . . . At the end of two or three hours a servant announces that tea is ready and conducts the gentlemen from their drinking to join the ladies in the drawing-room where they are usually employed in taking tea and coffee. After taking tea, one

[1] Seventy-five years later Mrs. Beeton thought it advisable to refer to the habit of gargling from, and into, finger-bowls. Like M. de la Rochefoucauld, she disapproved of the practice. She called it French.

23

generally plays whist, and at midnight there is cold meat for those who are hungry. While the game is going on, there is punch on a table for those who want it.

Invited to dine at more modest establishments in provincial towns, the Frenchman found that he was expected to present himself at 3 o'clock and to leave at 10—that is, just after supper.

References

J.H. ADEANE (editor), *The Girlhood of M. J. Holroyd*

J. D. BERESFORD (editor), *The Diary of a Country Parson*

FANNY BURNEY, *Evelina* (ed. by Sir F. D. Mackinnon)

—— *Cecilia*

—— *Diary*

OLIVER GOLDSMITH, *A Description of Various Clubs*

J. R. GREEN, *Oxford during the Last Century* (Ox. Chronicle and Berks. & Bucks. Gazette, 16 July 1859)

F. W. HILLES (editor), *Letters of Sir Joshua Reynolds*

CHRISTINA HOLE, *English Home-Life, 1500 to 1800*

C. E. MALLET, *A History of the University of Oxford*

C. P. MORITZ, *Travels Chiefly on Foot Through Several Parts of England in 1782*

F. DE LA ROCHEFOUCAULD, *A Frenchman in England, 1784*

MARQUISE DE LA TOUR DU PIN, *Journal d'une Femme de Cinquante Ans*

HORACE WALPOLE, *Correspondence* (Mary Berry, July 1790)

Crockford's, St. James's Street, now the Devonshire Club

III. Eighteen-Fifteen

FORTY years, tremendous years, went by. Both hemispheres were, politically, changed almost out of recognition, the habits of the upper and upper-middle classes in England hardly at all. Such, at least, may be the first impression; a closer inspection modifies it. There was one major innovation, which will be reached in due course. But even among the similarities a tendency to wobble can be detected, signs of unsteadiness, foreshadowings of that familiar phenomenon, a new world.

Though Miss Austen's novels are notoriously unaware of the great days in which they were written, though it is the rarest thing for any of her men to wear the King's uniform or any of her women to have a husband, son, or brother in Spain, France, or Belgium, her books will be everyone's choice as first witness. It is true that her fondness for contrasting rich and not so rich households makes her, for our purpose, highly useful. But she lived, materially and physically, a restricted life, and we cannot be sorry that she had rivals and contemporaries who lived very differently, and wrote stories wherein her details can be checked. Such is her renown that Miss Edgeworth and Peacock are, by comparison, neglected authors; but the Irish lady had a cosmopolitan upbringing and Peacock was a Londoner. Their careers, too, were in marked contrast to Miss Austen's swift, dazzling swoop, and for us, knowing the facts and the dates, it is difficult to avoid the impression, however fallacious, that theirs was a longer, if less intense, survey than hers. When Miss Edgeworth was born, *She Stoops to Conquer* had not been written, and she had the chance—from what we know of her, she will certainly have taken it—of reading *Jane Eyre* before she died. Peacock's first novel was published before *Northanger Abbey* and *Persuasion*, his last was later than *Adam Bede*.

Breakfast

The family still assembled at ten, after a couple of hours spent in walking, writing letters, reading, interviewing the servants, gardening, music, and other pursuits. Professional men continued to live near, if not positively over, their offices. With no train to catch, no bus to queue for, they walked to work; and this, by a mysterious but generally recognized.law, gave them plenty of time. Breakfast was thus a leisurely meal, less hurried but also less quiet than the rather grumpy, monosyllabic, and somehow suspicious gathering with which we usher in the day. There is a magnificently restless, strenuous, and agitated breakfast described in *The Absentee*. To the party at Lord Clonbrony's house in Grosvenor Square, already sufficiently distracted by her ladyship's rheumatism and his lordship's duns, there enters at a run Sir Terence O'Fay. The sanguine and high-spirited baronet makes a place for himself at table, asks for tea to drink, and regales the company with an account of his activities since rising. Being unable to find a coach so early, he had walked to Crutched Friars, near the Tower of London, in search of a certain solicitor, whom he had much annoyed by disturbing at breakfast; on leaving him he had found a conveyance and driven to Long Acre where dwelt Lord Clonbrony's chief creditor, a coach-builder, with whom he had another, and even stormier, interview. Sir Terence makes it clear that he considers himself to have done pretty well, and Lord Clonbrony assures him that he is 'very thankful' for the efforts made on his behalf. It would not be difficult to cite from other novels other breakfasts no less exhausting and full.

Sir Terence's interruption of the solicitor's breakfast cannot have been later than 9.30. Ten o'clock was still the hour for people of leisure and fashion; the rest of the world was beginning, from choice or compulsion, to lengthen the morning. Elizabeth Bennet, anxious about Jane, found the Bingleys assembled at 10; she herself, from her father's humbler establishment, had set out after breakfast and covered three miles on foot.

The truly Peacockian breakfast had to begin long before 10 if it was not to fill the entire day. At Headlong Hall, 'the seat of the ancient and honourable family of the Headlongs,

of the vale of Llanberris, in Caernarvonshire', the hospit-
able squire cherished an old custom:

> to have breakfast ready at eight, and continue it till two;
> that the various guests might rise at their own hour, break-
> fast when they came down, and employ the morning as they
> thought proper; the Squire only expecting that they should
> punctually assemble at dinner. During the whole of this
> period, the little butler stood sentinel at a side-table near the
> fire, copiously furnished with all the apparatus of tea, coffee,
> chocolate, milk, cream, eggs, rolls, toast, muffins, bread,
> butter, potted beef, cold fowl, and partridge, ham, tongue,
> and anchovy. The Reverend Doctor Gaster found himself
> rather *queasy* in the morning, therefore preferred breakfast-
> ing in bed, on a mug of buttered ale and an anchovy toast.

Peacock, of course, liked a bit of fun, but his evidence
should not be disregarded too readily. If he idealized food, it
was because he respected it. No man has ever described
meals more frequently, more lovingly, or at a greater length;
every few pages he began to feel hungry and to assume that
his reader must be growing hungry, too. Forty years later,
as we shall see, Borrow was served a breakfast, in a humble
Merioneth inn, which showed that the traditions of the
neighbouring county still lingered, and that Peacock had
exaggerated not at all.

We do not know what the Bingleys were consuming on
that morning when the eldest Miss Bennet surprised them
by her early call, pink cheeks, and muddy skirt. Indeed, if
their creator has a fault, it consists in a certain superiority to
gluttony, a slightly chilly enjoyment of the good things of
the table as opportunities for observing character rather than

for guzzling. Yet, for whatever reason, she drops her hints; and so, when William has to leave Mansfield Park at the startling hour of 9.30 on the morning after the dance, Fanny sees him off and then, creeping sadly back 'into the breakfast-room', cries unrestrainedly over 'the remaining cold pork bones and mustard' on her brother's plate and 'the broken egg-shells in Mr. Crawford's'. She has thirty minutes for grief. Then came 'the second breakfast'.

Except for those egg-shells, all the main dishes at Mansfield Park and at Headlong Hall seem to have been cold.

One might suppose that, rising at 11 from cold pork and the rest of it, our ancestors could have kept going for an hour or two, if not till dinner itself. It was not so. In London, they dropped into coffee-houses or pastry-cooks' between noon and 1 o'clock; in the country, the slightest exertion seems to have made them ravenous again. Following that noble breakfast at Headlong Hall—at which, it is true, they were the first to seat themselves, but of which, as Peacock noted, they 'enjoyed *les prémices des dépouilles*'—Mr. Escot, Mr. Foster, and Mr. Jenkinson walked to Tremadoc where, 'after inspecting the manufactures, and refreshing themselves at the inn on a cold saddle of mutton and a bottle of sherry, they retraced their steps towards Headlong Hall' and the principal meal of the day. The appetites of the three philosophers would not have struck Miss Austen as out of the way. When the Bertrams and their friends visited Mr. Rushworth to inspect his plans for embellishing his property, they left Mansfield Park soon after breakfast (about 11.15), drove ten miles, and reached Sotherton about 12.30. 'It was first necessary to eat, and the doors were thrown open to admit them through one or two intermediate rooms into the appointed dining-parlour, where a collation was prepared with abundance and elegance. Much was said, and much was ate.'

Luncheon

The habit of a midday snack was thus well established. What is new at this time, what is the innovation alluded to in the opening paragraph of the chapter, is the development of the snack, the legitimizing of it by a name.

The words nuncheon and nunch occur as early as the fourteenth century. Luncheon was a seventeenth-century form, with possibly a different *nuance* of meaning. Both expressions appear in various spellings, and seem to have suffered something of an eclipse, or at least of semi-desuetude, from Cromwell's time till a hundred years later. Johnson's *Dictionary* (1755) gives 'Nunchin: A piece of victuals eaten between meals', but defines Lunch and Luncheon as 'As much food as one's hand can hold'. When, once again, a word was wanted to mark the snack's development, the earlier form was resurrected. Miss Austen herself uses it in a letter written in 1808, and spells it 'noonshine'. In the course of the next few years, the old word, or words, gained a favour never previously known.

This brief account of what is now in everybody's vocabulary has been compiled, to the best of my ability, from the confusing and often contradictory details available in the more important dictionaries. The subject is not one which shows our lexicographers and etymologists at their best, and the adventures of the word are still obscure. One or two

points are worth mentioning as we move to firmer ground.
For example, the fortunes of the day were still so uncertain
in 1829 that the committee of Almack's Club felt it could
no longer maintain a fugitive and cloistered virtue and declared itself a supporter of 'lunch', adding that 'luncheon is
avoided as unsuitable to the polished society there exhibited'.
On the other hand the *New English Dictionary* (Clarendon
Press, 1903) observed that many persons were still regarding
'lunch' as a vulgar abbreviation. The verb 'to lunch' seems
to have achieved its first, rather hesitating, admission in
1832; reversing the usual progress, it began life below
stairs, in the servants' hall. 'Nuncheon' died, but much later
than most people believe. It was still in use in the rural parts
of Wiltshire, round Salisbury, in the last decade of the nineteenth century.

As far as my reading has taken me, I should say that the
first three occasions when the expanded meal and its resurrected name earned a place in fiction are these: Miss
Austen's *Sense and Sensibility* (pub. 1811), Miss Edgeworth's *The Absentee* (pub. 1812), and Miss Austen's *Pride
and Prejudice* (pub. 1813). In *Sense and Sensibility* the form
is 'nuncheon', and the suggestion is a rough and hasty meal
consumed by an impatient horseman while his mount is
being rubbed down by the ostler at an inn. Miss Edgeworth's
allusion, a year later, is more informative. A party of London maidservants, having accompanied their lady on a visit
to Ireland, are here seen on an excursion of their own to a
neighbouring village:

'. . . just the cast barouche like, as she keeps for the lady's
maids.'

31

'For the lady's maids! that is good! that is new, faith! Sir James, do you hear that?'

'Indeed, then, and it's true, and not a word of a lie!' said the honest landlord. 'And this minute, we've got a directory of five of them Abigails, sitting within our house; as fine ladies, as great dashers, too, every bit, as their principals; and kicking up as much dust on the road, every grain!—Think of them, now! The likes of them, that must have four horses, and would not stir a foot with one less!—As the gentleman's gentleman there was telling and boasting to me about now, when the barouche was ordered for them at the lady's house . . . they just drove out here to see the points of view for fashion's sake . . . and up with their glasses, like their ladies; and then out with their watches, and "Isn't it time to lunch?" So there they have been lunching within on what they brought with them; for nothing in our house would they touch of course! They brought themselves a pick-nick lunch, with Madeira and Champagne to wash it down. Why, gentlemen, what do you think, but a set of them, as they were bragging to me, turned out of a boarding-house at Cheltenham, last year, because they had no peach pies to their lunch!—But, here they come! shawls, and veils, and all!—streamers flying!'

Miss Edgeworth was a careful writer with a good knowledge of the fashionable world in England as well as Ireland. She visited England in the year following the publication of *The Absentee*, but from her letters she seems to have been uninterruptedly at home in Ireland for several years before. Either, then, the novelty of luncheon had now reached her country, or she was expanding an anecdote related to her in conversation or correspondence. She had a reverence for extracts from 'real life'—one of the many weeds sown and watered by her father—and was fond of asterisks and daggers drawing the reader's eye to 'A Fact' in a footnote.

No such label is attached to the passage just quoted. A note, however, seems called for by the unexpected word 'pick-nick'. It had been current for some time, but had always been used in reference to a habit practised on the Continent and not yet followed here. 'Originally, a fashionable social entertainment in which each person present contributed a share of the provisions; now, A pleasure party including an excursion to some spot in the country where all partake of a repast out of doors.' (*New English Dictionary*, 1909.) The application of the word to a meal in England first occurred about 1800, so that here again Miss Edgeworth, like a good novelist, was showing herself up to date. It is generally said that the mark of an early pick-nick was the contributory idea, and that this continued till 1870 at least. But by 1826 Disraeli could already write 'Nature had intended the spot for pic-nics', whilst Miss Edgeworth's landlord clearly used the word to indicate that the party had brought food with them. He cannot have been interested in their contributions, and there can hardly have been any; the hamper was presumably filled by the cook of the big house to which the maids belonged.

Readers will be more familiar with the last of the three instances. Jane and Elizabeth Bennet, returning home from London, are treated to 'the nicest cold luncheon in the world'. Their surprise, and the pride of their sisters who had prepared it, indicate that luncheon was something of an event in Mrs. Bennet's house, though she would not have

33

liked to hear us say so. The cloth was not laid, the meal was not served in the dining-room.

Mansfield Park appeared one year later than *Pride and Prejudice*, yet in her account of the trip to Sotherton, already quoted, Miss Austen refrains from attaching 'luncheon' or 'lunch' to what was obviously a luncheon party. To look for underlying significances in every line of text is a mistake easily made by commentators; but one may, perhaps, idly and unemphatically wonder if the popular revival of the old words was not beginning to look a little too sudden and complete, imparting almost a catchword air. During the past few years, writers far less fastidious than Miss Austen must often have avoided the use of 'definitely' and 'actually'. By the time these pages are in print, they may even, let us hope, be looking twice at 'frustration'. Provided, then, that we do not raise our voices, we shall do little harm in speculating whether the word 'lunch' may not have been passing through a period when it had ceased to be 'amusing' and might have been dethroned, if an acceptable rival had presented itself.

The application of a name to a habit already existing but hitherto unchristened may seem, at the time, no more than a convenience; but it is usually the effect of gentle pressure, of almost imperceptible compulsion. The informal midday snack had become more important and solid as, in spite of many wobblings, more men were eating breakfast a little earlier and everyone was dining a little later. Even on social layers where the notion of trade was still abhorrent, the industrial revolution and the ripples of the class war across the Channel were making their apparently insignificant marks. These marks have accumulated, numerous and gigantic; from the midst of them we may still spare a glance for Mr. Willoughby (*Sense and Sensibility*). He would have been greatly astonished to think that his 'nuncheon' at Marlborough was destined to become, in a century and a quarter, the principal meal of the day; he would have dis-believed flatly that his plate of cold beef and pint of porter would compare, in time, with the principal meal of the week.

Dinner

The aware, the astute, the hobnobbing Thomas Creevey knew very well that, to rise in society, a man must give the impression not of climbing but rather of finding, even of being helped up to, his own level. He seldom failed to note with gratification his slightest departures from the habits and conventions of the fashionable world; he cherished them as signs of sturdy independence, as proofs that nobody could call him a snob; and for the opposite reason we, too, cherish them as evidence of what was normal, of what he was being independent of and hadn't sold his soul for.

In two letters written to his wife in the first week of 1811, he remarks that he has taken to dining at 6 o'clock, adding that his friend, the future Lord Dudley, was alive to his foible. Eleven years later he was dining at 3.45; it was, he declared, 'much the best hour to dine at', but whether it recommended itself by convenience, novelty, or the presence of Brougham and sundry lords and ladies he does not precisely say. We should like to know, we are compelled to guess at, his reasons for varying his dinner-time, in the course of hardly more than a decade, by as much as two and a quarter hours. The change seems too great to be attributable to the war or the victorious peace; whatever its cause, it must be considered a sign of fluidity in the habits of the era as well as of the snares besetting our investigation. The Universities themselves floundered; undergraduates, even of one college, could dine at any time between 3.30 and 5.

There is other evidence that, at the very beginning of the nineteenth century, dinner was for a while eaten later than in the preceding and succeeding periods. From her *Journal* we learn that Lady Nugent, returning from Jamaica in 1805, found her friends dining at 6 in London and at 5 in the country. Mr and Mrs. Bolingbroke, the chief characters in *A Modern Griselda* (1805) usually dined at 6, and they were an ordinary, well-to-do, bourgeois couple moving in no very exalted circles.[1]

The introduction of the 6 o'clock habit seems to have been premature; with fair unanimity the novels of the

---

[1] The passage in question occurs near the beginning of Chapter 2, and illustrates a rather unexpected detail in the life of the time. It lies outside our subject but, in view of the obscurity into which the novel has now fallen, it seems worth rescuing. Mr. Bolingbroke apologizes to his wife for coming home half an hour late for dinner. She replies that he is an hour late. He, a man with brief experience of married life, extending over only one chapter, insists that he is right because 'I set my watch by the sun today'. He may have meant a sundial; he may have meant that, in his office (though we are not told if he had one), the position of the sun at noon was customarily checked in relation to a chimney or spire. In any case his creator, Miss Edgeworth, brought up in a 'scientific' household by a 'scientific' father, strongly implies that Mr. B.'s evidence, though contested by his wife, will convince the educated reader. London had then had public clocks for more than a century; soon they were to be illuminated at night. Street clocks must have been plentiful enough. Mr. B. ignored them. He was a steady man, and knew what he was about.

second decade indicate that 4.30 was the normal dining-hour of country gentlefolk. Mr. Woodhouse (*Emma*) dined at 4; but he was a man whose charm consists precisely in this, that never by word, deed, or thought had he seen any cause to depart from the habits and outlook which, in boyhood, he had taken over from his father. General Tilney (*Northanger Abbey*), a very different sort of man but equally incapable of adjustment, dined at 5 'even in the country'—a reminder that Londoners had ways of their own. There is, indeed, only one piece of evidence which is uncomfortable, angular, and hard to accommodate. Henry Crawford (*Mansfield Park*), visiting Fanny Price at her parents' house at Portsmouth, made a point of leaving 'when he knew them to be going to dinner, and therefore pretended to be waited for elsewhere'. In this he was both tactful and wise. The Prices were a numerous swarm, existing in cramped quarters and reduced circumstances; their table, as anyone might guess, was crowded, ill-served, and far from appetizing. So 'he went to while away the next three hours as he could . . . till the best dinner that a capital inn afforded was ready'. Although he no doubt ordered his meal, a table d'hôte service being then most unlikely, this long interval puts the Prices' dinner exceptionally early or the hotel meal exceptionally late; but what is perplexing to us was apparently simple to Miss Austen, and she withholds an explanation we should have been glad to possess.

In the main, however, the novels of the Waterloo decade are so well agreed on the dinner-hour, and those written by Miss Austen so widely known, that the reader may be spared the many accessible references. Ladies and gentlemen, unpaired in the reception-room and unplaced at table, continued to be left to their own contrivings; important strangers were doubtless guided to important chairs, unimportant strangers were apt to be left unheeded until, with every expression of delight, they could take the last, the suspiciously empty, the deliberately shunned and only remaining seat. In this, as will be noted, there is no change from 1780; and all the details of the meal and of the whole evening—the removal of the cloth, the mitigated retirement of the ladies, the qualified absence of the men, the wine, the coffee, the tea and cards and supper—seem to have remained virtually unaffected. All those little customs in which routine and freedom are, to our eyes, so curiously mingled, had persisted through forty or fifty years of major campaigns over half the globe, of social upheavals and commercial depressions, of restrictions on travel and outbursts of cosmopolitanism, through acute, protracted perils and sudden, utter safety, from Bunker's Hill to St. Helena, from *The Deserted Village* to *The Excursion* and *The Cenci*.

Supper

Supper then, like champagne now, was served without comment in the houses of the rich and fashionable, but in Miss Austen's world it is by no means inevitable, and is apt to mark a rather special occasion or important guest. The experience of the Reverend Mr. Collins (*Pride and Prejudice*) sums up the situation very conveniently. When he was honoured by a command to dine at Rosings, Lady Catherine de Burgh, after five or six hours of his company, saw no reason to delay his departure by hopes of supper, nor did he expect that she would. But when he was the guest of Mrs. Phillips, whose husband had been a clerk, he dined, and then he had a muffin with his coffee, and finally, after a game of whist, a hot supper of several dishes.

Creevey moved in the supper-eating circles. Rolling from house-party to house-party and filling ducal note-paper with accounts of ducal shortcomings, he lets us see what the guests expected, even if they did not always get it. Mr. Milbank, of Thorp Perrow, satisfied his standards—'excellent and plentiful dinners, a fat service of plate, a fat butler, a table with a barrel of oysters and a hot pheasant, &c., wheeled into the drawing-room every night at $\frac{1}{2}$ past ten'. It was not a set meal; it was, rather, a buffet to which the guests could turn as often as their dauntless appetites stormed back victorious from the previous round; and it went on for some time. It was over by 11 o'clock at North-anger Abbey but that, as the author tells us, was an early household. When the Bolingbrokes were staying quietly in the country with their friends the Granbys—Mr. Boling-broke will be remembered as the man who set his watch by the sun—supper seems to have trickled on till nearly 1 o'clock. Mrs. B., retiring to rest, found a note from her husband, signed T. Bolingbroke, informing her that he had left her. Always reliable, he dated it midnight. He can hardly have allowed himself less than forty-five minutes for writing the letter, clearing out of the house, and leaving a reasonable margin against Mrs. B.'s fatigue, indisposition, or boredom.

Before casting a last look back over the long day, we must glance at those people who, without a capable wife, attendant staff, and comfortable home to turn to, found themselves at a loose end. Since it was almost impossible for a lady, even if she tried, to be at a loose end, such people were usually men away from home or joined in assembly. They ate at coffee-houses. For the happy few there already existed White's, Boodle's, Arthur's, Brooks's, but the great era of clubs was still just ahead, and the coffee-houses remained what they had been for 150 years, the customary, obvious, and only meeting-places for men who had no, or too much, home life. They were of all kinds—quiet and distinguished, uproarious and crowded—and they tended to have their special clienteles, commercial, sporting, artistic, journalistic, colonial, maritime, theatrical, political. The age, however, was a versatile one. A cabinet minister might well be an author who owned an important collection of pictures, kept a sharp eye on his farms, had designed a new wing for his house, and won the Derby with a horse of his own breeding. The old, Elizabethan zest for all-roundness was not yet dead, and it would be an error to suggest that a man sought always the same company. Eminent or humble, scholars or aesthetes or tradesmen, they were all great readers of the newspapers which lay about the coffee-houses and formed not the least of their attractions.

The better his establishment, the greater the proprietor's difficulty in keeping it, even if he wished to, select. Sometimes a group of *habitués*, annoyed by the other customers, bought the premises and the business, which thus became a club. Sometimes they were driven out. Captain Gronow relates that the officers of the Foot Guards frequented a coffee-house at the bottom of St. James's Street—an indifferent house, but handy. 'Unseemly broils and quarrels often took place . . . caused mainly by the admission of (or rather the impossibility of excluding) Irish bullies and persons of fashionable exterior but not of good birth or breeding.' As a result, the Guards'. Club was formed in 'luxurious apartments in Pall Mall', the subscription being, at first, £5 per annum.

Meal-times in coffee-houses did not differ, of course, from meal-times in the home, and this digression would not perhaps have been necessary, and certainly not so long, were it not valedictory. Shops which specialize in the serving of coffee can still be found; the old idea still whispers, unmarked, above a hundred thousand *cafés*. But the coffeehouses have gone, will have gone a few pages hence, where we shall find their functions divided between whole blocks of clubs, public houses doubled in number, and the first, adventurous restaurants.

The day

We have now, for the first time, an opportunity to compare the divisions of the day in two separated periods. It is also an opportunity to warn anyone who may be expecting great and dramatic changes that he is watching a slowmotion picture.

Family breakfasts were still at 10 o'clock; but the solicitor in *The Absentee*, whose meal was interrupted at 9.15 or 9.30, observed the time-table of many busy men and of young people impatient of old ways. This lawyer's clerks were doubtless already at work; he himself would be free for his first clients soon after 11. It would be a mistake to make the further and easy assumption that his day ended at three. Even before he entered Parliament, Samuel Romilly complained of having to spend ten hours a day in the Courts of Justice; and from *Ennui* (another of Miss Edgeworth's novels) we learn that clerks in legal offices worked from 9 till 4 and again from 5 till 10. Those are long hours; and the two examples come from different ends of the same profession—the successful lawyer, soon to be Solicitor-General, and the humble copyist. Neither of them can have breakfasted later than 8 o'clock. Moreover, they carry in their wake a considerable trail of other people, not only the judges themselves but all the Court attendants, the jurymen, the witnesses, the litigants and their friends, as well as the households from which they had all set out. One must conclude that the solicitor was not in Court on the day when Sir Terence disturbed his leisurely, yet still comparatively early, breakfast.

But even in more genteel households where the old habits prevailed, there were signs, too, of greater activity in the hours before 10. During her visits to London in 1811 and the following years, when she stayed with her brother Henry while seeing her proofs through the press, Miss Austen found the mid-morning queues so tedious that she took to shopping at 9 o'clock, before breakfast. There is a particularly illuminating letter dated Thursday, 16 September 1813. 'Up and dressed and downstairs' by 7.30, she writes:

> At nine we are to set off for Grafton House [a draper's] and get that over before breakfast. Edward is so kind as to walk there with us. . . . We returned from Grafton House only

42

just in time for breakfast & had scarcely finished breakfast when the carriage came to the door. From 11 to ½ past 3 we were hard at it.

The passage repays study. She was able to add to this letter late in the day, but it is evident that, when there was a dinner engagement, she (and all the other voluminous correspondents of her era) had no time for writing save in those hours before breakfast. Her brother Edward accompanied her because a lady, at that time, never ventured out alone in London. The presence of an escort was not a mere concession to moral standards, it was a comfort, it was almost a necessity, in a city where there were still undeveloped areas of marsh and scrub, infested by footpads. Miss Burney's Cecilia saw nothing wrong in slipping out of the house in the early morning, unknown to her guardian, but she never dreamed of going without her servant. The duty of escorting a lady was thus something for which a gentleman had always to be ready; and, however pleasant, it was not negligible. The lady, escorted here or there, had often to be escorted back again, and on the occasion just mentioned we learn that Edward, while his sister and daughter matched ribbons and trimmings, sat on the draper's stool for three-quarters of an hour. Lastly, the reader will notice that, on that busy September day, there was no thought of luncheon or even a snack.

Miss Austen, like most ladies, was home by 3.30, but the shops were far from closing-time. All the people who, from 11 to 3, were busy attending on the gentry, were obliged to defer their own shopping till late in the day. The shop assistants themselves can never have shopped, their hours were far too long. At the old tobacconist's at the top of the Haymarket there is preserved an 'Instruction to Staff', undated, but attributed to 1800. It runs: 'Open the shop at 6 o'clock in the Summer and as soon as it is light in the Winter. Cleanse it and put all things in their proper place.' We must recollect that the Haymarket was then fulfilling the function implied by its name; like Covent Garden today, it was early astir. But the instruction cannot be altogether explained away by local conditions. At that same date, the old hat shop at the bottom of elegant St. James's Street was open all seven days of the week.

Some of the purely luxury trades fared better. Into the theatre bills and programmes of the Enthoven Collection at the Victoria and Albert Museum, there has strayed a card of invitation to an exhibition of pictures. It belongs to the year 1818, and it tells us that the canvases were on view for just the anticipated hours, 11 to 3. But art dealers have always been a small and chosen fraternity, employing few hands. There is no doubt at all that in spite of the short day of people of leisure, shop assistants worked twelve hours a day and more. Whom did they serve, in the high-class, fashionable, and expensive shops? I have not been very successful in suggesting an answer; nobody, as far as I know, has ever found the complete one. On the sinking of the social sun at 3.30 a crowd of satellites would be released, the shops would refill; yet still the hours seem longer than necessity or profit can have dictated. There is a little mystery here, not to be slurred over.

We have seen that the midday snack was not an innovation, but that the application of a name to it began to grow

44

in favour and to arrest the attention of observers. Moreover, the name was not a new one; it had been in fluttering, spasmodic use for a very long time, but now it stuck and, as the future was to show, stuck for good. The midday snack was becoming a midday meal. It was, as yet, something to be mentioned; slight formality attached to the serving of it; and most men, on most days, were content to make no more serious interruption than was needed for a sip of Madeira and a cake, or something of the kind. But the significance of this shy innovation is great, for it is undoubtedly the result of a rather earlier breakfast and a later dinner, and thus of a lengthening day. From the evidence of Peacock's novels and even of Miss Austen's, we might conclude that the added time was just one more hour to do nothing in. Miss Edgeworth is valuable in correcting that impression. She became early in life the unpaid bailiff and manager of her father's estate, and her stories are full of men engaged on the improvement of their property or finding it difficult to make both ends meet. Such men must have welcomed the postponement, even by half an hour, of the need to prepare for the evening in the middle of the afternoon.

They had no afternoon. They did not know the two halves of our working day, so similar in length and achievement, so different in sensation. Though luncheon is still, in the years under notice, a shy new-comer far from general acceptance, it marked the entry of a change in habits that cannot be called less than tremendous. To appreciate the results that were to flow from this timid beginning we must look forward a few decades, to the day when lunch became customary in most classes of society and dinner gained an

alternative title, 'the evening meal'. By that time the afternoon had been created or, rather, re-created.

At first sight one might suppose that the introduction of
an important hinge, at 1 or 2 o'clock, must have broken the
day; indeed, I have just referred to its two halves. But the
innovation worked in various forms. It postponed dinner, or
allowed it to be postponed, and men of business and affairs
came to realize that their wives, fortified by lunch, could
wait for dinner and that they themselves, if they ate a larger
breakfast, could spend eight or nine consecutive hours in the
office, interrupted only by the time given to a Maid of
Honour and a glass of port. Similarly their wives were free
of them for eight or nine hours at a stretch instead of four or
five; they had the house to themselves, they had a meal to
themselves, they had, like an exciting fresh toy, the afternoon to themselves; in spite of the example of the Court, the
figures of divorce rose steeply. For the more innocent men
of leisure there was the new, or the unrecognizably changed,
world of outdoor games. In the eighteen-fifties golfers were
beginning (so Mr. Bernard Darwin assures me) to find that
they could play two rounds and still be home for dinner. By
bolting their breakfasts they could be on the first tee as early
as 11 o'clock; their courses were only 12 or 14 holes in
length; and they could pause once, if not twice, at a well-
sited lunch hut or ginger-beer stall before resuming their
customary foursome. By 1840 Gentlemen v. Players and the
University match had become annual fixtures. By 1850
football clubs were multiplying in London, Lancashire,
and Yorkshire, in Wales, Scotland, and Ireland; in 1863
footballers of both codes met, drew up rules, formed their

respective organizations, and separated. The great edifice of Sport was taking shape. Lunch, with its postponement of dinner, was far from being the sole cause of all this activity, but it was a principal contributor. The reader, laying down the book and following in his thoughts the ever-widening ripples of lunch, may wonder if they have yet reached shore.

The fluctuations, during the opening years of the nineteenth century, in the hour of dinner—first later, then earlier, and then again later—were inevitably reflected in the theatres, but as the arrangement of the evening resettled itself, performances tended to begin at the old hour, 7 o'clock. For occupants of stalls and boxes, and the kind of dinner they were likely to eat and the pace of the conveyance they used, two hours must have meant a rush. Possibly, before going to the theatre, they dined a little early; certainly they would no longer have time to dress after dining; probably they arrived a little late. The theatre, though a great attraction to them, remained paradoxically a social rather than an artistic event. Among novelists who wished to emphasize the innocence and freshness of their heroine, there had long been, and still was, no device more favoured than a description of her first evening at a theatre, and her distress at being unable to hear, through the hubbub of late arrivals and general conversation, a word of the play. We are never allowed, as far as I know, to hear the shouts of remonstrance from the cheaper seats; yet then, as now, their occupants could stand up for their rights. When, in 1809, Smirke's new theatre at Covent Garden arose on the ashes of Holland's building, the management tried to recover costs by raising prices. For two months there were nightly riots, and during that time no lady could show her face in a box without being pelted with missiles of an unspecified nature.

If the day was lengthening, the night was not shortening. Vauxhall had not yet ceased to be smart, though its great era was ending; the subscription dances at Almack's (known to us, and bombed to earth, as Willis's Rooms) were now run, and thronged, by the best people, and there were, of course, rival dances for the merely better. The vogue of the gambling clubs must often have resulted in a shortage of men, for they were crowded by half the peerage, half the Cabinet, and half the ambassadors. White's and Brooks's were, in the years under consideration, being eclipsed by Wattier's; the greatest of them all, Crockford's, was about to open. To read Gronow's list of the members and *habitués* of that gaming house is, today, an astonishing and perhaps wholesome experience. The Duke of Wellington and Prince Talleyrand were among the patrons; a little later 'Disraeli and Bulwer Lytton displayed . . . the one his sable, the other his auburn curls', while in a corner of the room, 'snug and sly at his desk', was 'the old fishmonger himself'. In a few years he made over a million; 'one may safely say, without exaggeration, that Crockford won the whole of the ready money of the then existing generation'. But the poor deluded gentlemen got something more solid than excitement for their money, something with which they, and we, might end their day—a celebrated chef named Ude, a lavish supper, 'the best wines in the world', and all thrown in, with the furnishings and flunkeys of the palace in St. James's Street, free and for nothing.

EIGHTEEN-FIFTEEN

References

JANE AUSTEN, The Novels
——, *Letters* (ed. R. W. Chapman)
F. CUNDALL (editor), *Lady Nugent's Journal*
MARIA EDGEWORTH, *A Modern Griselda*
—— *The Absentee*
—— *Ennui*
H. H. GRONOW, *The Last Recollections*
SIR H. MAXWELL (editor), *The Creevey Papers*
T. L. PEACOCK, *Headlong Hall*

IV. *Entr'acte*. Twenty Years Pass

MISS AUSTEN made one of her heroines uninterested in music, another indifferent to flowers. These touches, so striking to us, can have caused her no concern. They do not advance her stories, they are not developed; and she was the last woman to mock convention or parade her audacity. Yet no subsequent novelist, as far as I recollect, has dared to invite sympathy for young ladies so brutish; as for the readers of the rawest works of contemporary fiction, accustomed to forgive their heroines all the vices, and indeed eager for the opportunity to do so, they may well be annoyed to find that, before they can stop themselves, they are shocked by girls as perverse as Elinor Dashwood and Catherine Morland.

In these two asides by the novelist we can see, if we choose, one of the last flickers of a disappearing world, of vanishing ages, of something which, having survived all the centuries, withered in the earnest and aspiring atmosphere of the nineteenth. It was as if, driven out by Romanticism, a nip went from the air. Whether the English benefited from the gentler zephyrs is another matter. We know that they were in for a hundred years of comparative peace, of complete freedom from fear of invasion; but they, of course, lacked that comforting assurance, and in any case went through a period of dislocation and adjustment, of trade depression and social unrest, offering many parallels to our experiences a century later. It was a time which, if not positively chaotic, was extremely complex. In his *English Social History* the Master of Trinity found it necessary to devote two and a half chapters to disentanglement of the influences and tendencies which pushed and tugged from the last days of George III till the death of William IV; of a survey covering six centuries, nearly one-tenth is taken up by the intricate picture of twenty-five years.

We cannot be surprised, therefore, that our subject should be thrown into corresponding disorder. Already our late Georgian ancestors have appeared far more erratic in their meal-times than are their great-great-grandchildren, and this impression will be greatly strengthened during the next few pages. Creevey has given us a glimpse of what we may expect. Invited by him to dinner, when did a friend knock on his front door? At 3.30 or 5.45? Nowadays a guest can hardly be more than half an hour too early or too late. During the reign of George IV he could easily be two hours out in his reckoning. Chance visitors must sometimes have been uncertain of the name of the meal at which they were assisting; and even formal occasions were conducted with a vagueness that must have strained the nerves of cooks. 'I arrived late at Mr. Bischoff's,' noted Henry Crabb Robinson in his diary, 17 October 1831, 'having mistaken the dinner-time by an hour. Of little moment this. I found a large party assembled.'

We have reached a point when, in all directions, the pattern changes. Luncheon, like the second centre of an ellipse, begins to elongate the day, though not in the way expected; forces (and not only those which led to the introduction of luncheon) are pressing existence into fresh shapes. There is much to watch, and we shall have to turn our gaze constantly from side to side as well as backwards and forwards. The twenty years between 1820 and 1840 offer, indeed, so few perches where we can rest without violent oscillation that, for a bird's-eye view, we shall have to hover and dart, always on the wing.

Of the main authorities consulted, and listed at the end of the chapter, one or two call for remark since the works quoted are not strictly contemporary. *Jane Eyre* is declared and (especially in its earlier chapters) has been accepted as largely autobiographical; the author was still young and there does not seem to be much danger in trusting to her recollection, even after an interval of fifteen years, of the habits of 1830. In assuming a similar reliability in *Cranford* I hope to have the sympathy and support of most readers. Both books are valuable in their freedom from metropolitan influences. A third provincial, Miss Edgeworth, needs a different excuse or none at all. Her records are contemporary and, though she lived in Ireland, she was a frequent visitor to England where the affection and number of her friends continued, throughout her long life, to grow. Her knowledge of polite society in London was probably much more intimate than Thackeray's or Dickens's, her power of observation little if at all inferior.

Breakfast

The older generation, like Miss Edgeworth and her friends, and the more conservative men of affairs, like Macaulay and his set, continued through both decades to rise at 7 or half-past, to read or write for a couple of hours, to breakfast at 10. Since even in Miss Burney's novels a young man would not always wait so long for his first meal,

Confectioner's Shop (*from an engraving c.* 1820).

and since the Bennets (*Pride and Prejudice*) breakfasted not later than 8.30, there is nothing very significant in the discovery that, towards the end of the reign of William IV, there was a growing tendency for younger people and simpler households to breakfast earlier. In Lytton's *Ernest Maltravers*, as late as 1837, an ambitious young man about town is clearly very proud of being able to say that he never breakfasts later than 'a quarter before nine'.

Compared with the other meals of the day, breakfast came through a trying period with wonderful imperturbability. Its principal change was that it went on getting better.

> Mr. Mac Quedy: Well, sir, and what do you say to a fine fresh trout, hot and dry in a napkin? or a herring out of the water into the frying pan, on the shore of Loch Fyne?
> The Rev. Dr. Folliott: Sir, I say every nation has some eximious virtues; and your country is pre-eminent in the glory of fish for breakfast. We have much to learn from you in that line at least.

The passage is from *Crotchet Castle* (1831); Disraeli, referring to this year or the next, commends English inns for their hot breakfasts, and seems to suggest that the ordinary housekeeper had not kept abreast of them.

There is no need to expand this comment. Breakfast was showing signs of moving back a little against the clock; it was becoming a recognizable affair of hot dishes, tea, and coffee, in place of the cakes and chocolate of fifty years before; and, as Victoria mounted the Throne, it was losing some of its social flavour and prestige. It had a rival.

Luncheon

The furtive snack was thriving like some poor foundling who learns that he is the bearer of an honoured name. As early as 1818 luncheon seems to have been served regularly between 1 and 2 o'clock at Bowood, the Lansdownes' place in Wiltshire. Such a habit was unusual; very few of the subjects of George III were anticipating our custom so closely. However, in the very same year that Creevey was supporting 3.45 as 'much the best hour to dine at', in the year 1822 there was appearing, in monthly parts, a work entitled *Real Life in London*. If I compare it to a guide-book to London written by the social columnist of an evening paper I may succeed in conveying an idea of the nature and quality of these collected, and connected, sketches. Being deliberately ephemeral, they contain much information omitted from more serious compilations; and since such commentaries were at that time popular and this particular series had a good reception, we may assume that the anonymous author was familiar with the scenes he illumined. 'Women, however, are not quite so irrational as men, in London, for they generally sit down to a substantial lunch about three or four; and if men would do the same, the meal at eight would be relieved of many of its weighty dishes.' To emphasize his point, that luncheon was a fashionable innovation, welcomed by the ladies but despised by the gentlemen, the writer goes on to say that even in those circles where hostesses had their way and dinner was delayed till 8, the gentlemen, rather than fall in with new-fangled notions, would arrive famished and fasting, having eaten practically nothing since breakfast. In these circumstances dinner naturally grew larger and lasted longer than ever, and supper disappeared. The stomachs of men like Creevey, dining one day at 3.45 and another at 8, supping one night and not the next, must have been enviably accommodating.

We have seen how, two hundred years ago, Lady Suffolk was insisting on dining at an hour which Pope declined to admit. Some readers will remember how, forty years ago, there were plenty of men who disdained to join their wives' tea-tables. So, in the twenty years under discussion, women led the way that men were eventually to follow. The divisions of the new day had, to our eyes, everything to recommend them. Yet they were the invention of ladies of leisure, and perhaps for this reason were very slow in finding acceptance among men of affairs and the families of the worlds of business and the country-side. These active people clung to the meal-times of an England which had not yet lost its American colonies or heard of Napoleon or fully grasped the significance of James Watt.

Thus began a domestic schism which was to last for a long time and has not yet been entirely healed. The day divided into two forms, a man's day and a woman's, and they ran on simultaneously and separate. We will look first at the ladies.

1821 As already mentioned, the Lansdownes, in their country house, were lunching from 1 to 2. I do not know what they ate.

1823 Miss Edgeworth, on her way to visit Sir Walter Scott at Abbotsford, stopped for lunch at Moulinan. 'First course, cold; two roast chickens, better never were; a ham, finer never seen, even at my mother's luncheons; pickled salmon, and cold boiled round. Second course, hot; a large dish of little trout from the river; new potatoes and . . . a dish of mashed potatoes for me; fresh greens, with toast over, and poached eggs. Then, a custard pudding, a gooseberry tart, and plenty of Highland cream—*highly* superior to lowland—and butter, ditto.' For this, she was charged six shillings. On arrival at Abbotsford she passed— she had no choice—into Scott's régime, back into the days of no luncheon, dinner in the middle of the afternoon, late supper, and all the rest of it.

1831 The same lady, being in London, attended a luncheon party of forty people. It was an unusual affair, not only on account of its size but also because a man presided, the Bishop of Llandaff.

1832 (approximately) In one of the early chapters of *Coningsby* two gentlemen, wandering round a large London house, open the door of a room where the ladies are lunching. The hour seems to have been about 2.45. They are invited to join the ladies and, with some apparent hesitation, they do so and are served with chicken pie with truffles, sherry, and 'confectionery'.

The idea of a set luncheon was slow to make its mark in the modest houses of rural districts. At Mrs. Reed's (*Jane Eyre*) dinner was over by three. Even so, luncheon is mentioned, but it can hardly have been more than the old-time snack. In *Cranford* nobody, not even the Honourable Mrs. Jamieson, ever lunched or could have lunched. 'From twelve to three are our calling hours.' One of Miss Mitford's villagers still 'rose at four in winter and summer, breakfasted at six, dined at eleven in the forenoon, supped at five, and was regularly in bed before eight'. She is, of course, presented as a survival, but the reader is clearly meant to be amused, not incredulous, much as we should be today by an old gentleman who persisted in paying afternoon calls in a top hat.

57

Provincial ladies were not more conservative than London men. In a letter to his sister, written in 1831, Macaulay mentions that Lord Althorp 'from his getting up, till four o'clock ... was engaged in the business of his office; that at four he dined, went down to the House at five, and never stirred till the House rose, which is always after midnight; that he then went home, took a basin of arrowroot with a glass of sherry in it, and went to bed, where he always dropped asleep in three minutes'. Macaulay's own day was similar, the difference of three hours at dinner-time being then negligible. 'I am very quiet,' he tells his sister again, in 1833: 'rise at seven or half-past; read Spanish till ten; breakfast; walk to my office; stay there till four; take a long walk; dine towards seven; and am in bed before eleven.'

Macaulay and even Althorp must have appeared as light weathercocks to Wordsworth who, at Rydal Mount in 1835, was still dining at 1, with tea at 6 followed by a light supper. The point, the common habit to be noted, however, is that none of these men ever thought of luncheon. During her visits to London, Miss Edgeworth always received a number of invitations to luncheon. In the years between 1830 and 1840 that sociable and conscientious diarist, Henry Crabb Robinson, lets hardly a day pass without a note of breakfast or dinner eaten in company; I have found only two mentions of luncheon, and on each occasion the word is used for a snack consumed at an odd hour on a disarranged day. In March 1836, when Walter Savage Landor came to breakfast with Robinson, they rose from the table at 2—the very moment that luncheon was ending at Bowood.

It would be far easier to quote another score of such con-

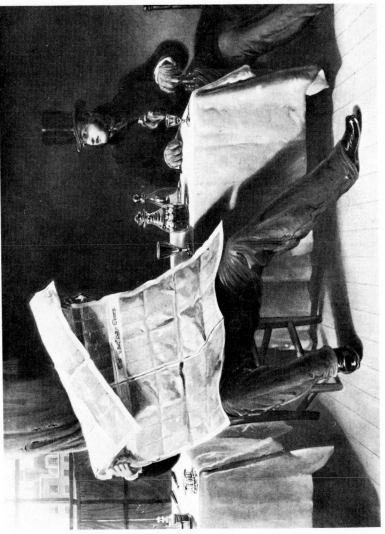

1. *Waiting for* The Times, B. R. Haydon (1831).

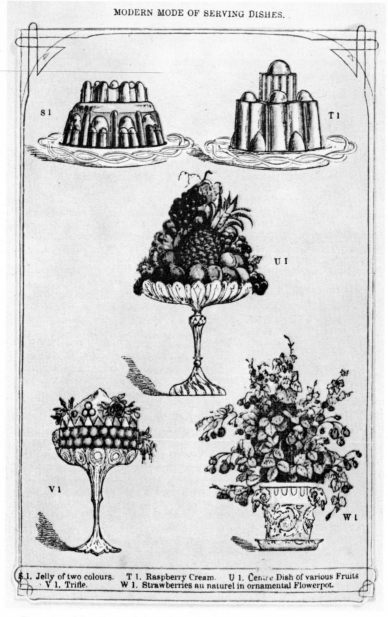

S 1. Jelly of two colours.   T 1. Raspberry Cream.   U 1. Centre Dish of various Fruits
    V 1. Trifle.   W 1. Strawberries au naturel in ornamental Flowerpot.

2. Reproduced from one of the colour plates in the first edition (1861) of Mrs. Beeton's *Household Management*.

3. *A Family at Tea*, artist unknown (c.1730).

4. *An Epergne*, drawing by George du Maurier, reproduced in
Punch, January 1880.

servative admissions than to find a single instance of a man who habitually sat down to luncheon. The resistance put up by the men was, too, as prolonged as it was strange. According to his biographer, it was not till 1853 that Macaulay yielded, and then only under compulsion of failing health, 'to the detested necessity of breaking the labours of the day by luncheon'. The view persisted, and is worth noting, that luncheon was a destructive rather than a recuperative force. 'Four in the afternoon,' Macaulay recorded with an almost audible snort, 'lunch hardly digested.'

Dinner

By now it will be plain that at this period of our history a Londoner might be found dining at any hour between 1 and 8. The argument that dinner at 1 and supper at 8, and luncheon at 1 and dinner at 8, were identical in all but name is tempting and easy. It is perhaps too easy. It will be attended to presently. Leaving it, for the moment, on one side, let us look at the meal still sometimes described today as 'late dinner'.

We find the principal innovation at once, before the dining-room is reached. At some moment early in the reign of William IV the practice of leaving the company to push its way in as best it could began to give place to more orderly proceedings. The change did not come about in a moment or everywhere. At first, the host would offer his arm to the most important lady, recommend his wife to the care of a viscount or ambassador, and consider himself rid of all further obligation. The remaining guests followed in the old, haphazard fashion; and if two men had matter for discussion or were friends whose paths too seldom crossed they would think it natural to sit together. They were free to do so; they did not, and could not, disarrange a table which had never been arranged, or disturb a balance which did not exist. The idea that the table should be surrounded by alternate ladies and gentlemen, like a diced girdle, had not yet taken hold; but, however restricted in its early stages, the habit of pairing off could not go very far without leading to pairs, to the sexes in equal numbers. The formal dinner-party, as we know it or knew it, is barely a hundred years old.

Though dinner might be followed by music, cards, conversation, or that extraordinary pastime of the age, the turning over of the pages of albums, there were nights and houses in which the hours brought, for the ladies, nothing but their coffee. They may have preferred it that way; the gentlemen, even if they arrived in time to be served with tea, must often have been far from amusing. In the reign of William IV, Besant tells us, they were fond of sitting on over their wine till midnight; the King himself, according to another authority, liked punch, sherry, and champagne with his meal and a couple of bottles of claret to himself during the afterglow. Much can be accomplished, given time; four hours were devoted to this performance, and His Majesty was sure, if and when he reached the drawing-room, to find the ladies of the Court, nodding perhaps, but still there. But the men of less exalted house-parties must sometimes have found an empty drawing-room, their less exalted ladies being already an hour in bed.

Their absence or departure might be the signal for another little orgy. In the opening years of this inquiry, years in which *Evelina* was being written, smoking had died out. Social historians have followed one another in repeating that it stayed out of favour for eighty years, not returning until, by a ridiculous but typical frolic of Fashion, it became smart and somehow patriotic to share the only comfort of our soldiers in the Crimea. It makes a pretty story; but there are aristocrats in Disraeli's novels who, twenty years before the Crimea, were ending the day with cigars, whisky, and half a dozen of their peers, all stowed away in a bedroom of the bachelor wing. As a witness Disraeli has his limitations; his time-sense is very imperfect, and he will make two characters meet at 5 o'clock, talk politics for an hour or so, walk from St. James's to Grosvenor Square to consult a cabinet minister, walk back to Piccadilly and there go their different ways just as five-thirty is chiming. But on the manners and habits of leaders of Society he is reliable enough. He studied them with the reinforced care of a novelist and an ambitious politician. His splendid gentlemen, surreptitiously puffing away in distant rooms at late hours, employed the technique of schoolboys because they knew that the smell of their clothes and hair might betray them if they smoked during the day; and so, insensibly, it seems to have become bad form to smoke before the small hours. Another contemporary novelist, describing a poor man smoking at his cottage door, sees no harm in his pipe, but clearly expects to shock us by pointing out that noon had not yet struck.

The Day

All sorts of features familiar to us were now appearing,

existing for a time beside other, older forms which they were to replace. Though their day had not yet come, the early restaurants were visible, usually foreign and small but occasionally foreign and large. There was a Café Royale (so spelt) in Regent Street in 1822, with peers of unspecified carat among its patrons. But the coffee-houses were good for some time yet, and in this same year was published a description of the Globe which would fit our Claridge's or Savoy. Already some coffee-houses, however, were developing the anaemia of the tea-shop, serving nothing more substantial than bread and butter and an egg. There were places, too, where maids dispensed nothing but coffee to no one but men; they were called coffee-rooms, a term with several senses. Similarly chop-houses, eating-houses, dining-rooms were designations implying social distinctions and, by misapplication, blurring them. Taverns were, perhaps, the most resistant, their clients singing catches and choruses as for three centuries past.

These places were for men. At an eating-house you could have a plate of roast beef, pork, or mutton for 6d., three potatoes for 1d., pie or pudding for 3d., bread 1d., porter or ale 1d., a shilling in all with 1d. for the waiter. At the London Tavern a good, but not wildly extravagant, meal cost a guinea, not counting the tip to the girl. It is curious to note that, contrary to present practice, waitresses were among the refinements provided at the smarter establishments, service by waiters being part of the roughness of the cheaper houses. Dinner at a club would cost no less and, since the pound or guinea included the wine, we can only wonder that it cost no more. Before Victoria's reign began, clubs were multiplying and were much used for breakfast and dinner; her reign ushered in the era of pubs.

A return to our strict subject and a summary of an untidy period may be simultaneously supplied by Anderton's Hotel in Fleet Street. Three dinners were served there daily, at 1, at 3, and at 5. Since there was a fixed charge of 1s. 6d., the meal may have been table d'hôte; but Londoners as a whole did not take kindly to restriction and much preferred to eat *à la carte*.

That bewilderment, which no effort of the writer's can hide or of the reader's can master, is not ours alone, and we may console ourselves in the good company of the more observant spirits of the age. In 1833 we find the accurate and practical Miss Edgeworth using, without note of exclamation, inverted commas, or any other sign of raised eyebrows, the expression 'luncheon-dinner'; in 1839 when things, from our point of view, were at their worst, De Quincey, deep in a major essay on Roman manners, was struck by the erratic modes of his own day and turned into a diversion lasting several pages. Then, unfortunately, he recollected himself, but not before he had thrown a brilliant and unique light upon our scene.

In 1700 a large part of London took a meal at two P.M., and another at seven or eight P.M. At present, a large part of London is still doing the very same thing, taking one meal at two, and another at seven or eight. But the names are entirely changed; the two o'clock meal used to be called *dinner*, whereas at present it is called *luncheon*; the seven o'clock meal used to be called *supper*, whereas at present it is called *dinner*; and in both cases the difference is anything but *verbal*; it expresses a translation of that main meal on which the day's support rested from mid-day to evening.

Upon reviewing the idea of dinner, we soon perceive that time has little or no connection with it; since, both in England and France, dinner has travelled, like the hand of a clock, through *every* hour between ten A.M. and ten P.M. We have a list, well attested, of every successive hour between these limits having been the known established hour for the royal dinner-table within the last three hundred and fifty years. Time, therefore, vanishes from the problem; it is a quantity regularly exterminated. The true elements of the idea are evidently these:—1. That dinner is that meal, no matter when taken, which is the principal meal *i.e.* the meal on which the day's support is thrown. 2. That it is *therefore* the meal of hospitality. 3. That it is the meal (with reference to both Nos. 1 and 2) in which animal food predominates. 4. That it is the meal which, upon a necessity arising for the abolition of all *but* one, would naturally offer itself as that one.

. . . When business was moderate, dinner was allowed to divide and bisect it. When it swelled into that vast strife and agony, as one may call it, that boils along the tortured streets of modern London or other capitals, men began to see the necessity of an adequate counterforce to push against that overwhelming torrent, and thus maintain the equilibrium. Were it not for the soft relief of a six o'clock dinner, the gentle demeanour succeeding to the boisterous hubbub of the day, the soft glowing lights, the wine, the intellectual conversation, life in London is now come to such a pass that in two years all nerves would sink before it. . . . Dinner it is— meaning by dinner the whole complexity of attendant circumstances—which saves the modern brain-working man from going mad.

. . . He, therefore, who dined at noon showed himself willing to sit down squalid as he was, with his dress un-

changed, his cares not washed off. . . . And to this vile man
a philosopher would say—'Go away, sir, and come back to
me two or three centuries hence, when you have learned to
be a reasonable creature, and to make that physico-intel-
lectual thing out of dinner which it was meant to be and is
capable of becoming.' In Henry VII's time the Court dined
at eleven in the forenoon. But even that hour was considered
so shockingly late in the French Court that Louis XII
actually had his grey hairs brought down with sorrow to the
grave by changing his regular hour of half-past nine for
eleven, in gallantry to his young English bride. He fell a
victim to late hours in the forenoon. In Cromwell's time
they dined at one P.M. One century and a-half had carried
them on by two hours. . . . Our English Revolution came
next; it made some little difference, I have heard people say,
in Church and State; I daresay it did; like enough, but its
great effects were perceived in dinner. People now dined at
two. . . . Precisely as the Rebellion of 1745 arose did people
. . . advance to four P.M. Philosophers, who watch the
'semina rerum', and the first symptoms of change, had perceived this alteration singing in the upper air like a coming
storm some little time before. . . . In Oxford, about 1804–5,
there was a general move in the dinner-hour. Those colleges
which dined at three, of which there were still several, now
began to dine at four; those which had dined at four now
translated their hour to five. These continued good general
hours till about Waterloo. After that era, six, which had been
somewhat of a gala hour, was promoted to the fixed station
of dinner time in ordinary; and there perhaps it will rest
through the centuries.

De Quincey, after arguing so closely, was rash to indulge
in that last prophecy; but readers who have noted that he
started with 7 or 8 as the dinner-hour and ended with 6

should blame the discrepancy on his contemporaries and not on the essayist. Men dined at 8 when the ladies had a say in the matter. At other times they all—widowers and grass-widowers, bachelor and stag parties—sat down not later than 6 and, for choice, earlier. At Brooks's, in 1828, the eight-shilling dinner was served at 4.30, and members were handed their bills at 7 sharp. There was also a supper at 11 o'clock; it sounds like a sustaining meal, for it cost six shillings and did not close till half an hour after midnight. The usual conflicting witness appears in the person of one of the most famous and fastidious gourmets of the time, Thomas Walker, who considered luncheon 'a joyless dinner' and dinner in the evening 'a cumbrous supper'. Being a sociable fellow he could not avoid them; but he was happiest, when left to himself, with dinner at 2, tea and buttered toast at 7, supper at 9.45, and bed at midnight.

It is hard to avoid a shock, to repress a start of surprise, on realizing that within a few months of the publication of Miss Edgeworth's last novel a man not much younger than Macaulay was lighting up an entirely new England, a very present England ignored or left unilluminated by his established contemporaries. Though Dickens is usually cited as a witness of the Victorian era, *Sketches by Boz* and *Pickwick* belong to the reign of William IV and they had been followed, before 1840, before our twenty years ended, by *Oliver Twist* and *Nicholas Nickleby*.

For my own sake, as well as that of the reader, I have held back Dickens's evidence from its earlier and proper place in the chapter and kept it till now. It seemed to me that a paragraph embracing Ernest Maltravers and Alfred Jingle,

Helen and Nancy, Contarini Fleming and Wackford
Squeers would present almost equal difficulties of perusal
and composition. Yet such is the confusion of the times that
Dickens's testimony, when it comes, is powerless to create
any great disturbance. Sharp customers like Ralph Nickleby
(office hours, 9.30–5) were quick to see the advantage of a
business lunch at 1.30; his friend, Sir Mulberry Hawk,
seems to have dined at about 7.30; but all the habits of these
bad men are obviously set in opposition to those of decent
folk. The money-lender's man, Newman Noggs, breakfasted at 8 and had his dinner at 2, if his employer was back
by that hour. Meanwhile the wealthy Cheeryble brothers,
in the same book, always dine at 2, though they saw nothing
inconvenient in postponing the hour, to mark a celebration,
to 5.30. On ordinary days their next meal was at 6, and they
called it tea. When John Browdie came to London and put
up at The Saracen's Head, 'the usual furniture of a tea-table
was . . . flanked by large joints of roast and boiled, a tongue,
a pigeon-pie, a cold fowl, a tankard of ale, and other little
matters of the like kind'.

The book *Nicholas Nickleby* brings out very clearly the
parallel and contrasted existence of two ways of living, the
old and the new, going on simultaneously. It does not show
us what happened when they converged, when men like
Ralph Nickleby, returning to the office after lunch, paid
a business call on men like the Cheerybles and found them
engaged, for the next hour, on the principal meal of the day.

During these twenty years the feature of London life
least impressed by the vagaries of the natives was, as usual,
the theatres, their maximum variation being no greater than

an hour and a quarter. Neither Drury Lane's 6.15 (1828) nor Sadlers Wells's 7.30 (1830) displays much concern for the habits of the world of fashion. In 1834 afternoon concerts were beginning at 1.30; if we suppose that the public was considered, the hour shows that lunchers were still an insignificant minority. In 1840 a performance at Drury Lane was billed for 8 o'clock, but it seems to have been an exceptional evening, with 'refreshments under the supervision of M. Verrey of Regent's Street'. On another occasion patrons were warned that they ran the risk of losing their seats if they were more than half an hour late. But generally, and significantly, playbills continued not to commit themselves to any definite hour for the rise of the curtain. One might have supposed that the pre-telephone generations were driven to a reliable exactitude in their engagements and entertainments. On the contrary, they shunned it.

References

ANON., *Real Life in London*
G. L. APPERSON, *Bygone London Life*
C. BRONTË, *Jane Eyre*
T. DE QUINCEY, *The Casuistry of Roman Meals*
CHARLES DICKENS, *The Pickwick Papers*
—— *Nicholas Nickleby*
BENJAMIN DISRAELI, *Coningsby*
J. C. DRUMMOND and A. WILBRAHAM, *The Englishman's Food*
MARIA EDGEWORTH, *Helen*
—— *Life & Letters* (ed. Augustus Hare)
MRS. GASKELL, *Cranford*
J. HAMPSON, *The English at Table*

TWENTY YEARS PASS

Lord Macaulay, *Life & Letters* (ed. G. O. Trevelyan)

M. R. Mitford, *Our Village*

Bulwer Lytton, *Ernest Maltravers*

T. L. Peacock, *Crotchet Castle*

H. C. Robinson, *Diary, Reminiscences, and Correspondence* (ed. Thomas Sadler)

G. M. Trevelyan, *English Social History*

V. The Eighteen-Sixties

AT the end of the last chapter we left two coexistent worlds, one clinging to the habits of its grandparents, the other shaping a day not unlike its grandchildren's. At all times the old and the young have to rub along together, divided by fifty or sixty years, but Victoria inherited a social family ranging, in its habits, over a century and a half.

The old, or the old-fashioned, are bound to lose and disappear; during the first half of the nineteenth century, however, they put up, in particularly hopeless circumstances, an exceptionally stubborn fight. Headed by acceleration, the features of our world were emerging, yet there were plenty of people, of all ages, classes, and counties, who went on ignoring the changes or regarding them as no business of theirs. At the stage now reached in our story, they still formed, as far as may be guessed, a majority of the population; yet we must raise our hats to them not in salutation only but also in farewell. We shall see them again from time to time, and wave and smile; but they can no longer be of use to us and must—poor, dear souls—be dropped.

These observations are no sooner made than, once again, they raise doubts and entreat modification. In the novels listed at the end of this chapter and covering a span of twenty years, the changes in the arrangements of the day hardly keep pace with the far greater alterations in the general atmosphere and outlook. In the earliest of them,

Anne Brontë might well be showing us, through very different eyes, the world of Jane Austen. In the latest, Mrs. Henry Wood describes the way of life which formed the fathers of many people not yet past middle age. But as the picture unfolds in slow motion, jerks and jumps are so smoothed away that, often enough, the only traces of them remaining are to be found in those passages with which the author padded out his narrative and the reader has little patience. Besides holding as deep a social significance as any novel of the period, Mrs. Beeton's *Household Management*, published in 1861, provides a more energetic jolt.

As far as meal-times are concerned there are, in *The Tenant of Wildfell Hall*, only two details which would not have fitted naturally and easily into *Emma*, or even into *Cecilia*. One is a reference to lunch, an item in the ladies' day; the other is, as evidence, still less emphatic and more doubtful. When Lord Lowborough, an abstemious man stopping in a convivial house, deserts the after-dinner decanter and joins the ladies, he is reproved by his wife for his intrusion. But since he bored her to death we are left wondering whether he had, in fact, broken a convention; for when another and more popular man presently followed him, he was received with smiles, bright eyes, and a tucking in of skirts on sofas. Both men, in the old way, got their cups of coffee; the others, arriving at 10 o'clock, were offered tea which had stood for half an hour.

Breakfast

Already, in 1840, breakfast was becoming more substantial, earlier, and less social, and the tendency spread and crystallized until, by 1860, the meal had a pronounced menu of its own and a character which had little of the family likeness shared by dinner and lunch. In one of his novels, Disraeli seems to suggest that the virtues of the new breakfast should be credited to innkeepers rather than to housewives; and in most people's minds it has always had, and still retains, a masculine quality. As early as 1854, as far away as Bala in Merionethshire, the White Lion fortified its guests against a wet Sunday morning with 'pot of hare; ditto of trout; pot of prepared shrimps; dish of plain shrimps; tin of sardines; beautiful beefsteak; eggs, muffin; large loaf, and butter, not forgetting capital tea'. Not all inns were so generous, and Borrow, who had remembered to put on his white shirt and to take his Prayer Book out of his satchel, was moved to remark, 'What a breakfast!' and again, 'There's a breakfast for you!' before turning to the little freckled maid to ask her age.

Yet in the home, where it had once been an occasion for entertainment and hospitality, it now began to acquire, in its seriousness of purpose, the anxious, earnest, and upright lineaments of the Prince Consort. While friends, though still occasionally invited to breakfast, no longer dreamed of dropping in, members of the household could never, save under doctors' orders, drop out. The new state of affairs calls for rather prolonged comment.

After the now-famous breakfast had been laid but before it could be consumed, the entire family and staff spent ten minutes in the incense of its dishes, either looking at it and guessing the secrets of its hisses, pops, and crackles, or kneeling to inhale the furniture polish and inspect, through open fingers, the carpet's design in crimson and blue. The prayers, like the meal that followed them (kedgeree, sausages, cold pheasant, and the rest), laid a firm foundation for the Victorian day, but it is useless to deny that a formerly happy gathering had become a rather anxious one. Anxiety for the lie-a-bed child or guest, anxiety for the hot-faced, breathless maid, anxiety even for the amateur reader and hymn-player—all these anxieties led to a silent meal, with frequent surreptitious glances at the clock. Anxiety lay thick until dispersed by the banging of the front-door and the departure, for eight or nine hours, of the provider of the splendid breakfast and the well-found home. When that moment arrived, the lightening of spirits was eloquent enough, yet the dutiful children of that generation, conscious that the past hour had been overcast and never questioning their love for their parents, would sometimes put the blame for their uneasiness on Family Prayers. They did not know that that fine institution had not checked the gaiety of preceding generations and was not checking theirs. They could not know that a fiercely competitive and ambitious age was the cause of the hour at which they had assembled, the character of the meal they had consumed, and the care they had taken not to annoy papa.

In such a household—it was by 1870 the normal middle and upper middle class household—breakfast was at 8 or 8.15 and its punctuality was utter. Punctuality was a salient feature of the age, the accepted sign of a host of Christian virtues. The breadwinner would leave for the office at about 8.30 although, as he grew older, he might be content to see his sons depart at that hour, allowing himself a few minutes more with *The Times*, the *Morning Post*, or the *Standard*, and expecting the family to remain in their places while he read aloud the more anxious items of news.

A kind of urgency surrounded the meal, and everyone was expected to recognize and contribute to it. Even the ladies and the younger children, with no reason to leave the house for an hour or two, were accustomed to breakfast in boots. A novel published in the eighteen-sixties introduces us to a man who breakfasts alone in his bedroom, wearing a dressing-gown. To us, the start of revulsion is not spontaneous and, if achieved, comes slowly; but contemporary readers must have recognized him immediately for what he was, the villain. During the next thirty or forty years the children of those readers would have reacted almost, if not altogether, as directly to the novelist's device. What we call the Victorian breakfast persisted, as the British breakfast, in very many homes up to the turn of the century and in some cases up to the First World War. Many of us saw it die; but the obituary notices were few and contained no account of its birth and adolescence. Even now, too, if its body lies a-mouldering, its spirit goes marching on. About eggs and bacon for breakfast there still lingers, for many honest men, something of the sanctity of the Union Jack and Stratford-on-Avon.

Mrs. Beeton's first book, appearing in 1861, acknowledges the existence of breakfast but does little more than suggest, in the few lines devoted to the subject, various ways of trapping the head of the family into consuming odd bits of cold meat disguised as rissoles. Subsequent editions were not slow to adjust themselves; their powerful menus enable us to see what a good breakfast was, and also when Englishmen began to demand it. That demand was significant, marking yet one more new world, the growth of a commercial age, the first cold-shouldering of leisure, the stigmatizing of contented acceptance of inherited means and status, a lengthening of the day, a competitive acceleration, an added departmentalizing of family life, the abstraction, both mental and physical, of the husband and father. It is possible to see in the British breakfast a link between the decay of taste which everywhere, but especially in England, accompanied the progress of the century and the quadrupling, in the years dividing Waterloo and Sedan, of our national income.

Most offices opened at 9 o'clock, and for houses on the edge of London or in the developing suburbs the hours given above would need adjustment. Country dwellers, though quick to appreciate the new menu, saw no reason to adopt the new hours, and preferred to breakfast at 9 or even 10 o'clock unless there was some point in being energetic—a Meet, for instance. Trollope and Miss Yonge do not expect us to think any the worse of a man because he has not rushed out of the house, his tongue still busy with fragments of ham and marmalade, at 8.30. In London, it was different. When Dickens tells us that Mr. Fledgerby breakfasted at 10 o'clock, he hardly needs to add that he wore a Turkish cap for the meal. We know at once that he is a bad man.

In both town and country, tea was drunk, and muffins were a common and popular kickshaw. When, occasionally, the ghost of the British breakfast appears today, it bears no muffins with it, yet they had a long day. I can remember them always being served—well buttered, in a hot dish—at breakfast in an old-fashioned club in 1913 or 1914. Beside them a pot of blackcurrant jam would be posted; the mixture was delicious. Muffins for breakfast must, I think, have been a casualty of the earlier war then impending. Muffins for any meal seem to be an unrecorded casualty of the last war. Of the famous brotherhood the crumpet, sometimes stony, sometimes rubbery, alone survives.[1]

Luncheon

A long time has passed since up-to-date novelists, like Miss Edgeworth and Miss Austen, first noticed luncheon—fifty years, in fact. The reader may recollect that, soon after, he received encouraging accounts of the meal's steady advance in the reign of George IV. But male influence and the conservative element were still strong, and that sturdy non-luncher, Macaulay, was only one of a large opposition. Lunch remained less a set meal than a form of refreshment which, like a drink, a man accepted or declined according to his tastes and habits. Thus the Duke of Wellington (thirty years Macaulay's senior) took luncheon, but Metternich, spending three days at Strathfieldsaye in 1848, did not. On the whole, however, men (especially men high and low in the social scale) agreed in leaving luncheon to the women. Gentlemen in the City, like Ralph Nickleby and his friends, were more adaptable, seeing in the meal a focus, not an interruption, to their business.

By 1849, when *Shirley* appeared, lunch was still, or was

[1] Prolonged and fruitless search in London and the Home Counties lured me into downrightness; I should have known better. A muffin has recently been seen, in Towcester, Northants.

often, an improvised snack collected rather hurriedly for the entertainment of acquaintances who called—we do not know how innocently—in the middle of the day. 'This sort of impromptu regale, it was Shirley's delight to offer any chance guest'; cold chicken, ham, and tarts made up 'a neat luncheon'.

The passage seems to put luncheon back where it was in the days of *Mansfield Park*. But Charlotte and Anne Brontë are unsatisfactory witnesses, contradicting themselves from page to page. By contrast, a note on Luncheon in the second volume of *The Family Friend*, published in 1853, instils immediate confidence.

> This meal is admissable only when either the interval between the breakfast and dinner is very prolonged, or when the quantity of food taken at breakfast is very small. The lower classes, as well as the children of the higher classes, dine early, and thus with them luncheon is unnecessary and accordingly not taken. Not so, however, with adults of the middling and higher classes; with them, either from business or other causes, the practice of dining late has become general, and, with such, luncheon becomes a necessary meal. It should be taken about five hours after breakfast, and though called by another name it may be considered a light dinner, taken to allay the cravings of nature, but not entirely to destroy the appetite.

Later in the same decade Mrs. Beeton offered partial corroboration of this view. She does not attach much importance to luncheon, her long book contains only eight and a half lines of practical hints for it, and she leaves us uncertain whether childless women are entitled to the meal.

It should be a light meal but its solidity must of course in some degree be proportionate to the time it is intended to enable you to wait for your dinner and the amount of exercise you take in the meantime. . . . In many houses where a nursery dinner is provided for the children about one o'clock the mistress and the elder portion of the family make their luncheon at the same time from the same joint, or whatever may be provided. . . . The more usual plan is for the lady of the house to have the joint brought to her table and afterwards carried to the nursery.

One catches in these comments a disparaging note, a metropolitan ring; it is sounded more loudly still by that arrant Londoner, George Augustus Sala. When he spoke scornfully of people who were 'too proud to dine at the patriarchal hour' of 1 o'clock, he was far from being an old fogy; he was thirty-one.

Let us look at the country. In the Edmonstones' comfortable house (*The Heir of Redclyffe*) lunch was a daily occurrence, at 1 o'clock or nearly. Trollope's evidence is a good deal less firm than Miss Yonge's. He tells us of a *déjeuner* at noon, of a man lunching at (apparently) 2 o'clock, of men and women who dine at the old hours and never think of lunching, but chiefly he tells us nothing. His evasiveness and silences are disappointing; yet negative testimony, sufficiently pronounced, can lead to positive conclusions. If so faithful a chronicler says little, we should perhaps deduce that there was little to say.

Though the Edmonstones of Hollywell might lunch, their vicar's meal, eaten only a very little later, was called 'early dinner'; the good man had no late dinner save on the evenings when he was invited to the big house. Elsewhere in the story another clergyman, after conferring with his wife, decided that his new patron must be asked to dine, and at 6 o'clock. 'Won't that put you out?' asks the young baronet, displaying the 1853 brand of delicacy. 'Don't you always dine early? If you would let me, I should like to join you at tea-time.'

We can see, then, that lunch was struggling in London, and that in the country it was a matter of choice and, to some extent, of social standing, but not a matter of course. As late as 1866 an article entitled 'Morning Visits' appeared in the magazine *London Society*. When Mrs. Beeton talked of morning calls or visits she was, rather surprisingly, clinging to the old meaning, of calls made before dinner. But the writer of the article gave the words our sense. She tells the story of a certain Lady B— who, living in Scotland, devoted 'the whole day' to paying calls—a recognized habit in remote districts where, once the roads were dry, the carriage ordered, the horses harnessed, and the old coach-man dressed, it seemed a pity not to dispose of as many ac-quaintances as possible. Realizing that, in the course of her round, she would be glad of refreshment, she so timed her visits as to reach Castle C— at 2 o'clock. There she con-fidently but mistakenly expected to be offered lunch. The story, with its echoes of *Mansfield Park* and *Shirley*, indicates Lady B—'s luncheon hour but leaves us uncertain whether the occupants of Castle C— lunched earlier or not at all. Without this information the anecdote must have been, even for contemporary readers, almost pointless. The whole passage breathes discouragement and chaos.

Right at the end of the period under review, in 1869,

Mrs. Henry Wood comes forward with some fairly definite evidence. She shows us a solicitor of good standing who daily, at 1 o'clock, mounted the stairs from his office to his home above and joined his family at luncheon. At that hour his clerks, too, went out, but to eat dinner, since it was the principal meal of their day. The managing clerk went out with them, to what he called luncheon. He wished to make the juniors believe he dined in the evening, although in fact he did not; the social implications of his little pretence still survive.

The terms were used with a precision which would have pleased De Quincey. On one occasion when the older solicitor is at lunch, the author is careful to tell us that, as he was leaving town that evening, 'it was in point of fact his dinner'. On another day his son and partner, having to travel to a station near Birmingham by a train due at 6, dines before leaving London and, except for two glasses of brandy and water at his hotel, takes nothing more that day.[1] No

[1] Mr. Bede Greatorex, the traveller in question, had no choice between dining before leaving home, or at the inn after arrival. It is true that local confectioners were in the habit of sending boys to sell buns at carriage doors, but the first station buffet (Messrs. Spiers and Pond, at Farringdon Station, on the Metropolitan Railway) had only just made its appearance, in 1866. The innovation was successful and rooms, let out to catering firms, were soon provided on platforms at the more important provincial junctions. Special meals were served for, special halts were made by, long-distance trains. There was a famous 'twenty minute lunch' at Swindon; there was a similar timed meal at York as late as the nineties; I do not know when the custom died. The next step was the refreshment basket. This (also introduced by Messrs. Spiers and Pond) made its appearance in 1871, on the Leicester–Trent service—half a chicken, ham, bread, butter, cheese, and a pint of claret or stout, all for 3s. The first dining-car, between Leeds and London, ran in 1879.

aspersions are cast on the *cuisine* of provincial hotels, and we are left to wonder that a man who did not go to bed till after 11 should think that, if a meal eaten at 3 p.m. were substantial enough to deserve the name of dinner, he might not eat again. The incident suggests that, by the third decade of the Queen's reign, the backbone of the country was showing a certain rigidity. But, rigid or not, it was now being turned daily in the home, at 1 o'clock or thereabouts, towards the dining-room and lowered on to a chair for no 'impromptu regale' but for a regular meal. A late-morning caller might be asked to join the family at table, but we do not hear of friends being specially invited for the purpose and pleasure of lunching. Yet, as the reader may recall, Miss Edgeworth visiting London forty years previously could have lunched out two or three times a week.

Why did luncheon drop out as a social occasion? We can only surmise, once again, that what was at first an agreeable novelty lost its attraction, and that for a long time it was a sick meal, on the danger list. The ladies nursed it through its weakly adolescence. The men, whose lengthening days should have recommended it, would willingly have let it die. Those inveterate diners out, Dickens and Thackeray, seldom if ever mention a luncheon engagement in their correspondence; and though Ralph Nickleby was allowed to lunch in 1839, no such weakness appears, twenty-five years later, in Mr. Veneering and his associates, men with a stake in the country. Standing at Birch's counter, gentlemen in the City lunched off a glass of sherry with a rock-cake or a couple of biscuits; and if the less robust of them reached, day after day, the end of their tether, we do not hear of them usurping their wives' privileges; the ladies, though better fed, retained their old monopoly of swooning. In return for his hunger a man might, by suitable allusion, extract looks of awe from his family during the evening, but only on Sundays would he weaken. Even then he often protested, yet, still protesting, sharpened the carving-knife. To the eyes of his watchful children he should have appeared a superior, but seemed merely a different variety, of being.

Dinner

The Tenant of Wildfell Hall and *The Book of Snobs* both appeared in 1848, yet Helen Huntingdon's day is much nearer to Evelina's than to Thackeray's. No one can hesitate for a moment in choosing between the two versions.

Thackeray makes it clear that there were already two ways of dining. When at home he dined about 6 o'clock; Dickens preferred some half an hour earlier; these seem to have been the usual and favourite hours of busy men who could eat when they wished. The meal was solid and simple, the courses few. We see the Duke of Wellington, then in his eightieth year, dining at his club 'quite contented with the joint, one and three, and half-pint of sherry wine, nine'. Thackeray notes, too, that bachelors and widowers were finding cigars a substitute for feminine society, thereby disproving the legend that the smoking habit was spread by the campaigners of Inkerman.

Meanwhile the ladies had not lost their impetus, they were still pressing forward in the lead, and indeed, as we shall see, they were finding the going rather easier. Gentlemen in evening dress making their way on foot, between 7 and 8 o'clock, to stucco-fronted houses on one or other of Mr. Cubitt's estates, were enlivening the streets and pleasing the novelist's eye. On the entertainment awaiting them Thackeray's verdict was less favourable. The party, in his view, was always too large; he begs, again and again, for a company not more than ten in number—'a man and woman may look as if they were glad to see ten people'—but he clearly knows that his counsel is one of perfection and will not be followed. In a competitive age hospitality was being pressed into service and becoming an excuse for ostentation. 'Dinners', he observes, 'are given mostly in the middle classes by way of revenge.' His pleading had no effect. On the contrary, even he can hardly have foreseen the dinners lying a few years ahead, dinners he lived only just long enough to sit and shudder at.

His complaints were not new. A campaign for simpler meals and fewer guests had been begun ten or twelve years earlier by Thomas Walker and Abraham Hayward, men who, interested merely in civilized existence, made cooking and eating the subject of long, serious, sensible essays which still repay reading. They, in their turn, were inspired by another table-philosopher, Brillat-Savarin, whose *Physiologie du Goût* had appeared in 1826. The Frenchman wished to limit the company to a dozen. Walker's ideal party was six or eight; guests, if not acquainted, could then be properly and intelligently introduced, conversation was easy and intimate and, with decanters and dishes on the table and within reach of all, attendance could be cut down to a minimum. Walker makes it clear that Mrs. Beeton did not invent the huge, creaking, top-heavy dinner-party; she found it. Twenty-five years before her book was published, he was writing of 'the practice and example of the rich and ostentatious, who constantly keep up a sort of war-establishment, or establishment adopted to extraordinary instead of ordinary occasions; and the consequence is, that, like all potentates who follow the same policy, they never taste the sweets of peace—they are in a constant state of invasion by their own troops'. The repeated thrusting of side-dishes in his face he resented as an almost personal affront. He was deeply mortified if, at one of his parties, anybody had to ask for anything, even for it to be passed to him. It showed that he, as host, had been lacking in foresight.

As the years advanced from 1850 to 1860, Thackeray's dinner-hour moved from 6 to 6.30, to 7, then to an occasional 7.30 or even 7.45. An hour earlier, Dickens kept his distance; in 1855 we find him asking Wilkie Collins to join him at his habitual hour of 5.30, and in 1866 a similar invitation to Browning begs him to be punctual at 6.30. Other professional men, less famous but no less industrious, kept a like routine. Their office hours were usually from 9 to 5.30, differing by only a half-hour or so from what they are today; but these men dined as soon as work was over. Their wives were awaiting them at home, and not at a friend's house for conversation and a drink; and they passed their evenings, whether alone or with old friends invited, just as their parents and grandparents had done, with chess or backgammon, needlework and reading aloud, solos and duets and choruses. Steady-going, comfortably off, pursuing a sedentary calling, such Londoners had existed for many generations, and we have caught occasional glimpses of them in previous chapters. But now they were multiplying out of all telling, and they provided a ballast, out of sight and often forgotten, to the rather top-heavy society above, or at least around, them. Nevertheless, they were moving with the times. Their day, it will be noted, was persistently lengthening.

It was not to them that the young and pretty Mrs. Beeton addressed herself. She aimed at another world, the prospering, scrambling, climbing world of merchants, manufacturers, financiers, and politicians. When the first part of her large book appeared in 1859, eight and a half lines were devoted to lunch, a similar paragraph sufficed for breakfast, but 251 dinner menus were set out in full. No comment can be more illuminating than these figures, no description can do justice to those menus. They must be seen to be believed; and since, as they proceed month by month through the almanac, choice becomes ever more embarrassing, we will return to the beginning and reproduce her suggestions for a dinner for eighteen guests in January.

FIRST COURSE

*Mock Turtle Soup
removed by Cod's
Head and Shoulders*

Stewed Eels

*Vase of
Flowers*

Red Mullet

*Clear Oxtail Soup
removed by
Fried Filleted Soles*

85

MOVABLE FEASTS

ENTRÉES

Ragout of Lobster	Ris de Veau aux Tomates	Cotelettes de Porc à la Robert
	Vase of Flowers	
	Poulet à la Marengo	

SECOND COURSE

Boiled Turkey and Celery Sauce	Roast Turkey. Pigeon Pie	Boiled Ham
	Vase of Flowers	
	Tongue, garnished. Saddle of Mutton	

THIRD COURSE

Charlotte à la Parisienne		Pheasants removed by Plum Pudding		Apricot Jam Tartlets
		Jelly		
	Cream	Vase of Flowers	Cream	
		Jelly		
Mince Pies		Snipes removed by Pommes à la Condé		Maids of Honour

All the carving and helping was done at table, guests assisting; and sometimes, if not always, the host and hostess

86

faced one another across the narrow, not the long, way of the board.

The elaboration of such a meal, the physical strain of simultaneously serving so many dishes, watching so many plates, and tossing the ball of conversation to so many guests proved too much even for some Victorians, and a *diner à la Russe* began to win favour, the dishes being accommodated on the sideboard and handed round by the staff. The relief to the lady and gentleman of the house must have been immense, to the stomach not so great. A summarized form of Mrs. Beeton's suggestions for such a dinner in July is sufficient to show that the new freedom was employed to offer more rather than less:

    2 soups
    10 kinds of fish
    4 entrées
    6 hot joints, assorted
    4 cold birds—quail, duck, turkey, and chicken
    7 sweets
    Dessert and ices

Mrs. Beeton adds the note that 'Each dish may be considered a course.'

What an army of retainers, what an array of warrant officers, non-commissioned officers and men, what discipline, what parade-ground drillings, what ballet-like and balanced weavings must have been needed for such repasts, whether orthodox or merely *à la Russe*! What tempers in the kitchen, what tears in the scullery! From old ladies and gentlemen we can still get first-hand accounts of the dinners of the last Victorian decades, and they were tremendous enough. Nobody, alas, is left to tell us how he chewed his way through an evening in the sixties.

But without his help or Thackeray's we can recognize the age for what it was—competitive, snobbish, parvenu, purse-proud, vulgar, earnest, and indefatigable. They must have been, to borrow Byron's word for a social lion, 'endless' people. Many of them—to be more precise, the rising middle and upper middle class Londoners—were also the first, or nearly the first, arrivals in a new enclosure in the social order, created and fenced by their wealth. They had had a job to get in, they were having a job to get out, and they meant to make it as difficult as they could for others to get in or out. Nobody enjoyed half as much as they did the sneers at Sir Gorgius Midas and Mrs. Ponsonby de Tomkyns with which George du Maurier, week by week, sent up the sales of *Punch*. Some of the ladies, daughters, and granddaughters of those wives who, in every previous chapter, have been pushing towards a later dinner-hour and pulling their reluctant gentlemen after them, were beginning to wonder where they were getting to. We hear f them sometimes, when their husbands were booked for a civic banquet, dining thankfully by themselves between 2 and 3 o'clock and finishing with food for the day.

Still, they had won again, and as usual they were careful not to let the men know. ('A woman,' as Miss Austen once observed, 'especially if she have the misfortune of knowing anything, should conceal it as well as she can.') Members of Parliament, leaving the benches almost deserted from 7.30 to 9.30 and pressing into their new dining-rooms, were convinced that there at least, at St. Stephen's, they ordered their own lives. At home, out of consideration for the narrow sphere of their womenfolk, some of them even refrained from mentioning politics at all. Yet those obedient house-keeper-wives and those bullied housekeeper-daughters had, with their mothers and grandmothers, revolutionized the men's day. Helped, of course, by industrial and economic forces but consistently hindered by their husbands and brothers, they had doubled the active hours from four or four and a half to eight or nine.

Though each lady was by now regularly conducted into dinner by a gentleman, evidence suggests that even on important nights no special effort was made to provide a lady for each man; and so the main procession was apt to be followed by two or three dejected males hung, before the long evening had properly opened, with a placard of insig-nificance. For all its civilizing influence on table manners, the introduction of the pairing-off habit was, for them, a disaster.

House-parties in the country, being peopled with Lon-doners, are naturally quick to copy the ways of the capital: and now, at last, Trollope's chronicles demand a hearing. In *Doctor Thorne* (1858) we see Frank Gresham, previously instructed by his hostess, offering his arm to Miss Dunstable and taking her in to dinner—or, as the phrase then ran, taking her out. But though he would sit next to her, we are not safe in assuming that they were told where to sit or that the table was planned. In *Framley Parsonage* (1861) Trol-lope describes a similar dinner-party where, after the prin-cipal gentleman had taken 'out' the principal lady, 'there was no management apparent' in the placing of the other guests at table.

Men no longer followed the retreating ladies. Only too heavily aware that he was expected to propose to Miss Dunstable, young Mr. Gresham was at any rate spared the ordeal of trotting off behind her, and could keep his place at table, playing his part as a relaxed and claret-drinking man. When, later, he reached the drawing-room with the rest, they found tea awaiting them. For more than twenty years, men of taste had been taking coffee after dinner, and the position is a little obscure. Trollope's novels of this period, the Barchester period, suggest that, at mixed parties, coffee was still the monopoly of the ladies, and tea the after-dinner cup for men; yet at male parties, like the big dinner given by the Duke of Omnium at Gatherum Castle when all the guests were men, coffee was served, not tea. Both tea and coffee were falling rapidly in price, ceasing to be luxuries, and losing any snob-value they may have possessed, and the fight was a fair one. We are so accustomed to regard ourselves as a nation of tea-drinkers that some people may be surprised to learn that the import of coffee contested the lead as late as 1875. Then tea, having at length overhauled its rival, made such progress that, for a long time now, the quantity reaching our shores has been, and in spite of rationing still is, six times greater than that of coffee. As a consequence, a slight social distinction now adds its flavour to the two infusions. In well-to-do establishments, tea has almost entirely lost its place after dinner and at breakfast.

The metropolitan habits of the Big House had their parallel in the neat villas of the hamlet where, helped perhaps by improving communications, the hours of retired service men, doctors, and sprightly maiden ladies grew ever closer to those kept by their brothers and cousins in offices in town. Dinner was at 5 or 5.30, and it was still often followed, towards bedtime, by a meal that might be a small supper, a good tea, or one of the numberless forms of light refreshment. As the long evening drooped and nodded, the cakes and sandwiches, the urn and decanter, the mere opening of the door, must have been wonderfully reviving.

The great ones, like the Duke of Omnium, the Loftuses and the Proudies, dined at 7 or 7.30, and dined very slowly. The Duke's party, already mentioned, lasted for hours; when it was over, and even before, the guests rose from table, were helped into their coats, and drove or staggered home. His Grace had retired long ago, to bed or his library. When, on the occasion of Mr. Harold Smith's lecture on Papua and the Moluccas, the Bishop gave a little dinner at 5 o'clock in an hotel near the hall, he failed (to Mr. Smith's annoyance) to conclude the meal by 7; and the audience had to await, with what patience it could muster, the promised entertainment.

The Day

A couple of illustrations and three comments are all that is needed to fill in the already detailed picture.

On the threshold of our period and in the always conservative life of a university city, the Schedule of Professorial Lectures at Oxford for the Lent Term of 1854 reveals a day of six hours, from 10 until 4, uninterrupted by any break for luncheon. A lecture at 9 in the morning and two classes held by the Aldrichian Professor at 8 in the evening are the only projections from the regular pattern. No dons and no undergraduates, of course, would be in lecture-rooms continuously, but it is evident that many or most of them had breakfasted by 9 and had their next serious meal after 5. Such a day at such a date and in such surroundings has a reasonable appearance and shows the scholastic world moving with the times. It still, however, keeps its distance from the great world. Since our main business is with men and women who, without a thought of Oxford or Cambridge, are setting the pace, the next illustration shows the other extreme in time and in occupation.

In Book I, Chapter XI, of *Our Mutual Friend*, Dickens has left us an exceptionally precise account of the day of a successful business man in 1864. The liveliness of the description, even for Dickens, is very marked; no author not absolutely sure of his ground could exhibit such gusto; and the passage deserves quoting for reliability as well as enjoyment.

The world got up at eight, shaved close at a quarter past, breakfasted at nine, went to the City at ten, came home at half-past five, and dined at seven. Mr. Podsnap's notion of the Arts in their integrity might have been stated thus. Literature; large print, respectfully descriptive of getting up at eight, shaving close at a quarter past, breakfasting at nine, going to the City at ten, coming home at half-past five, and dining at seven. Painting and Sculpture; models and portraits representing Professors of getting up at eight, shaving close at a quarter past, breakfasting at nine, going to the City at ten, coming home at half-past five, and dining at seven. Music; a respectable performance (without variations)

on stringed and wind instruments, sedately expressive of
getting up at eight, shaving close at a quarter past, breakfasting at nine, going to the City at ten, coming home at half-
past five, and dining at seven. Nothing else to be permitted
to those same vagrants the Arts, on pain of excommunica-
tion. Nothing else To Be—anywhere!

Not every business man could set out for his office as late as
10 o'clock. This marine insurance broker was not Everybody, he was Somebody; his world was important, if less
important than he supposed. His hours may have been easy,
the significant thing about them is that they were regular.
What is ridiculous to us is the rigidity of Mr. Podsnap's
mind, not the rigidity of his habits. To Dickens one was as
big a lark as the other; it is hard to say which he finds the
funnier.

Even after Victoria had been reigning for a quarter of a
century the English still retained Creevey's enviable adapta-
bility, dining without discomfort at 5.30 on one day and at
8 o'clock on the next. Yet, though the process is slow, the
day was beginning to assume once again a set pattern, and
one contrasting sharply with the last previously discernible
pattern of some fifty years before. Miss Austen could
describe a society which was, on the whole, still undisturbed.
The subsequent agitation took a long time to subside, and it
was left to the pioneers of Portman Square to re-create order
out of chaos.

With the return of a general pattern, numerous details
fall easily into place and loose ends allow themselves to be
knotted. We can see that the Act of 1826, permitting the
establishment of joint-stock banks, had given an immense

stimulus to the business of banking; it is broadly true to say that all banks, as we know them today, are the result of the Acts of 1826 and 1833, the Bank of England alone excepted. There had thus arisen 'a situation already foreseen by Stendhal—the emergence of a society dominated by bankers; such a society usually develops a craving for ostentation'. In Cubitt and post-Cubitt symmetrical houses where they led their symmetrical lives, a correct and purse-proud generation formed with ardour what I have called a pattern but which was in reality something new and rather different, a standardization of existence. With the same steady tramp as the regular hours, there came (replacing Chippendale, Hepplewhite, and Sheraton, substituting discourse for conversation) the heavy furniture, the carpets and wall-papers which set Morris in revolt. Whereas, too, in recalling that earlier period, one likes to think that Miss Austen's heroines found a Turner, a Girtin, or at least Morland mezzotints in the stately homes of their bride-grooms, one feels more certain in guessing what their grand-daughters of 1850 looked for—a Prout, a Copley Fielding, or engravings after Landseer.

Some students of the eighteen-fifties have pursued the argument yet further, suggesting that women, who had once relied on a man's muscles, then his club, then his sword or pistol for their protection, now felt no security unless their husbands were, or at least looked like, bankers. To men of average appearance and to their tailors, nothing was easier than compliance with the ladies' wishes. To those ladies the death of the old Duke, in 1852, did not mean the end of an era, for the era had ended long ago. It can have meant little but an occasion for lip-service. The forty settled and peaceful years which they owed to him had become the natural order of things, owed (except on Sundays) to nobody. None but the brave deserves the fair? Instructing their maids in the proper treatment of master's silk hat, they must have thought Dryden a barbarian. The Crimean War and the Indian Mutiny possibly shook but did not change their views.

Meanwhile the theatres continued to open at 6.30 or 7 and, since even *King Lear* had to be provided with 'a new and farcical' curtain-raiser, they had little margin. Mr. Podsnap, we may be sure, waved them away with one of his sweeping gestures. It was their business to know that he dined at seven. It was not his business to know that the majority of theatre-goers had high tea at 5.30. 'If they do (not that I admit it) the fault lies with the sufferers themselves.' In an attempt to make the best of all worlds, some managers offered, on payment of a deposit, to keep stalls and boxes till 9 o'clock. The chances of resale at that hour must have been poor, and the expedient was presumably the accompaniment of a half-empty house.

References

Mrs. M. I. Beeton, *Household Management*
George Borrow, *Wild Wales*
A. Brontë, *The Tenant of Wildfell Hall*
C. Brontë, *Shirley*
Charles Dickens, *Our Mutual Friend*
—— Letters
The Family Friend, vol. iii (c. 1853)
A. Hayward, *The Art of Dining*

London Society, vol. x (1866)
G. A. Sala, *Twice Round the Clock*
W. M. Thackeray, *The Book of Snobs*
—— Letters
Anthony Trollope, *Barchester Towers*
—— *Doctor Thorne*
—— *Framley Parsonage*
Th. Walker, *The Original*
Mrs. Henry Wood, *Roland Yorke*
C. M. Yonge, *The Heir of Redclyffe*

VI. Afternoon Tea

THE growth of business and businesslike habits, steadily
justifying the ladies and pressing the dinner-hour farther round the clock, was not well received by the stomach.
English internal engines, designed for refuelling every four
and a half hours, begin to labour when asked to run for six
hours at a stretch. Once again wives and mothers took the
situation in hand and found the remedy. They invented
Afternoon Tea. Behind this simple statement there lies,
however, a complex story, political, industrial, and fiscal.

Many books, dry and watery, have been written on the
history of tea in Great Britain; encyclopaedias devote long
articles to it. Since our subject is not Tea but Afternoon
Tea, there is no need to set forth details so readily accessible
elsewhere. But the whole is inescapably a setting of the part,
and some reference to the rampant story, from the time of
Cromwell until the accession of Victoria, must frame our
theme and tint its background.

The English, or at least the London, public was first
offered tea in 1657, being advised to drink it for medicinal
reasons rather than for pleasure. Like most southern or
eastern commodities of that time, tea had been travelling
through Europe for a number of years before reaching our
island, and among the countries where it had been well received was Portugal. Five years after its introduction here,
a Portuguese princess became Queen of England. Catharine

was already a tea drinker, the Court dutifully followed her example, and from that moment tea, whatever its ups and downs elsewhere, was firmly established in English favour.

It was very dear, 60s. per lb. being paid for it in 1666. Either from its costliness or from the fashion of China, whence it came, it was drunk very weak. Sometimes dropping to 6s., sometimes rising to 40s., and generally averaging about 15s.; cursed as the ruin and defended as the amiable solace of the race; always being drunk by the natives and commented upon by foreign visitors; brewed in every home from the palace to the hovel; for ever in trouble and for ever triumphant, tea fought its way through the eighteenth century and emerged as the national drink. Few, however, were the social reformers who hymned its slow victory over ale. When, early in its career, tea became the monopoly, as an import, of the East India Company, it had thereby attracted to itself the disapproval of the Puritans, persistent and jealous foes of that privileged body; and the shadow of disrepute continued to hover. There were plenty of reverberators, before Cobbett, to return Johnson's thunder, the artillery on both sides was well matched and it is only history's irony that has kept alive, long after their roars have died away, the echoes of Cowper's tiny gun. Eventually the verdict of the early Puritans was reversed by their distant descendants, the Temperance Reformers of the nineteenth century, and tea was accorded moral support and became a virtuous drink.

All through the eighteenth century its popularity grew; in cottages it was drunk all day long, the leaves being used more than once. Yet how could poor people, how could any but the richest, afford it? The answer was supplied by the smugglers, who found tea a profitable adjunct to silk, tobacco, and brandy. We, who have dropped the tea from our luggage, may smile at the lawlessness of those days when an army of coastguards patrolled but failed to protect the countless coves and inlets round our shores; but it was an accepted business then, and only a few detached observers, like Horace Walpole, saw anything comic in members of the Board of Trade 'wallowing in contraband wines, tea and silk handkerchiefs'. The caves of England were full of untaxed luxuries, and so were the crypts of country churches. But even of smuggled tea the price was still too high for the poorer clients. For them the tea had to be mixed with sloe, liquorice, and ash-tree leaves.

For nearly 200 years our tea came from China. All the noted addicts—Queen Anne, Johnson, Lamb, Hazlitt, and the rest—drank China tea. Borrow's host, the old gentleman 'who knew Chinese, but could not tell what was o'clock', had acquired his strange lore by study of the characters on tea-pots, tea-chests, bowls, and wrappers. Even if he had wished to do so and no matter how much tea he had bought, he could never thus have learned a Hindu language. But in 1833 the East India Company was deprived by Parliament of its monopoly of the China trade. The Company had had warning of the change in 1813; its experiments in growing tea in India, already begun, were extended and hastened during the twenty years' interval; and in 1839 tea from India was, for the first time, auctioned in London. It was no cheaper than China tea; its flavour was unfamiliar; there was nothing about it to attract the public, and the public was not greatly attracted. For a long time 'China' continued to be a synonym for tea. Indeed, the struggle between India and China tea resembled and coincided with the match between tea and coffee. In both cases the first named won in the end, but only after a hard fight. Queen Victoria's Jubilee saw China tea still in the lead.

At that first auction in 1839 Indian tea fetched 16s. to 34s. per lb. Whatever, then, her hopes from competition, the housewife was no better off for the moment. Yet it was at this same moment or soon after it that relief began to come, on a scale and with a rapidity that competition alone could not have provided. In 1846 Free Trade triumphed, and its beneficent effect upon prices suffered not at all, as far as tea is concerned, by the repeated and sympathetic appearances, as Chancellor of the Exchequer, of a tea addict, Mr. Gladstone. The duty, which had been 2s. 3d. per lb., dropped to 6d. by 1865, and would have reached that point earlier but for the Crimean War; the annual consumption of tea rose from 1·22 lb. per head of the population to 3·29 lb. in the course of thirteen years. The pretty, and locked, little tea-caddies, from which the lady of the house doled out, in a screw of paper, a few precious leaves; the miniature tea-pots, the cups to match—all these disappeared. There was no more need for economy. Tea was cheap, and many other things, too. The chatelaine grew appreciably lighter.

In private, as well as in the public and popular Tea Gardens, millions of people had drunk tea in the afternoon without inventing afternoon tea. The credit for this innovation has been given to a Duchess of Bedford, and it is true that she seems to have discerned new possibilities in the tea parties held, by the Bluestocking ladies and others, after dinner; she gave her tea parties earlier and less formally, *al fresco*. But as an institution in the home, as an occasion not for dressing up and shining but rather for being dull and comfortable by one's own fire, afternoon tea had to wait until, as I have tried to show, successive Chancellors made it practicable and the domestic time-table made it desirable.[1] It was, at first, an affair of the nursery rather than the boudoir, the good mothers' escape from the dilemma of either sending the children straight to bed on top of one of Mrs. Beeton's family dinners, or keeping them up past their proper bedtime. Afternoon tea provided a meal suitable for children and an hour and a half for its digestion. Then, when the serious business of the evening set in, they could 'be packed off (as it is supposed)' to the night nursery, 'but really only to the staircase, down which they slide during the dinner-time, waylaying the dishes as they come out, and fingering the round bumps on the jellies'.

Some years ago I wrote to a lady of great age and unimpaired faculties, begging her to finger and sort out her recollections of the still dewy teas of her childhood. Her letter, in a hand as clear and flowing as her thoughts, is dated 10 January 1944, when she was eighty-eight.

> You have given me a real poser of questions which, however, has caused much chat, and any elderlies who have come in have been well interrogated as to their faithful memories. There was so much nursery life (downstairs at stated times)

[1] From Victoria's accession onwards, one gets occasional glimpses of tea, even of bread and butter, consumed in the afternoon. They are very rare, the partakers eminent, the dinners apt to be ceremonial and late. Still, the idea had been born.

and it would be difficult for you to realise my early days in a small house at Marlborough Hill. A move took place to the Finchley Road in 1864, larger house and nice garden.

I know that, when I was ten, I always had nursery tea after coming home from school. I had had my dinner there. This would bring the date to 1867, and I can remember our Mother coming up to the nursery for a cup of tea very often; so that looks as if she did not think it was right to have it made for herself alone, or it may have been that the staff was small—much was sacrificed for the nursery department in those days in many families. I remember her breakfast at 8, bacon & eggs. I have heard her say that she had quite a light lunch brought in on a small tray. There was a hot meal at 6–7, three courses, when Father returned from the City.

As the family grew the four eldest came down to break-fast by 8 to the minute, and then lunch was laid in the dining room for 1 p.m. But still I cannot recollect seeing teatrays about except when friends came or visitors were staying in the house.

Sunday was a great day. Breakfast 8.45 for the bread-winner's sake. At 1.30, hot dinner—joint, fruit tart and custard, and (best of all) dessert after. Dessert was invariable, I am sure, for Sunday. I know two old women who still cannot think it is Sunday without the table being cleared and finger-bowls put on, with apples, nuts or oranges according to season. Poor dears, they have to forgo them now! Then came afternoon tea in the dining-room at 4.30 and cold supper at 8. This ended Sunday.

The invitations to dinner parties were not later than 7.30, and very often 7. The old maid who now looks after me went out to service when she was twelve years of age. Her recol-lections are a *good* breakfast at 8, High Tea with fish or meat at 5, and cake and cocoa at 9. This was only 54 years ago, but in a country house. She asked me if I had ever heard of Donkey Tea. Tea was so expensive that her father's mother made it for her children to drink—toasted bread put in a Jug and boiling water poured on it, then left for some time before straining off.

Well, all this for you to read and really not a bit of good; but among all the books here I cannot find out when tea lessened in price, for that was the difficulty 80 years ago. Now you will be tired, and so is my writing hand.

On the strength of a sentence in a letter written, on 16 February 1680, by Madame de Sévigné, the innovation of taking milk in tea has been credited to Madame de la Sablière. The passage has been misread. Milk was going through one of its periodic phases of favour with the doctors, it was the fashionable 'cure' for everything, and Madame de Sévigné, being as usual worried about Madame de Grignan's health, recommended a course of it. Having a notion that her daughter disliked milk, she pointed out that the taste could be disguised; for instance, 'Madame de la Sablière prenoit du thé avec son lait; elle me le disoit l'autre jour.' That is a very different thing from adding milk to tea. The Chinese have always drunk tea without milk, and for a long while their habit was naturally followed; the flavour of China tea is at all times extremely delicate; it must have been barely perceptible when, owing to the cost, the pot was stinted. I do not know who first thought of weakening it still further, but little silver jugs, matching the tea-pot and the other items, began to form part of the tea-sets of the days of George I. They were cream-pitchers, and for a long time their appearance was far from being automatic. The numerous pictures of tea-trays and tea-tables produced during the next hundred years seldom, as far as my studies have gone, reveal jugs likely to have contained milk or even cream. In the painting here reproduced there can be observed, reading from left to right, sugar bowl, plate of 'fingers', caddy, cup, sugar tongs, hot water jug, plate of spoons, slop basin, and, on its heater, the tea kettle itself; except for the missing cream or milk, a very possible table today. The handleless Chinese cups are worth noting. Though not invariable, they were common at that time (c. 1730), and the anonymous artist has shown three different methods of dealing with them.

From the position of those sugar tongs one might argue that they had or had not been used. Sugar or other forms of sweetening had been popular almost from the first, I think; yet already, by the time this picture was painted, far-sighted mothers were warning their daughters that a love of sugar, and indeed of cream, would be recognized by watchful bachelors as a sign of ill breeding. It is a curious belief, curious in its origin, its persistence, and its survival, amid a holocaust of class-distinctions, as a mark of a small section of society. Even today the barmaids at railway stations can scarcely be restrained from dropping a lump in the cup; the traveller who likes his tea unsweetened is made to understand that he is one of a very troublesome and cranky minority.

The chapter should not close without emphasis being laid once again on the restriction of the first afternoon teas to the nursery population. The ladies, though not always good or even bad mothers, seem to have been rather slow to realize the possibilities of a private and delicate version of the

meal, essentially feminine as it appears to be, and its gastro-
nomic delights, its friendly intimacies, its confidential
exchanges were all left undeveloped and unappreciated.
Long before 5.30 the flicker of the latchkey, and the
thunderclap of the front door, the returning figure of Mr.
Podsnap, irritable with hunger and relying on a good dinner
at 7, must have cast a shadow over the house, introduced an
apprehensiveness into the air; and in such an atmosphere
afternoon tea might be taken but hardly savoured. Perhaps
the ladies unconsciously felt, moreover, that having come so
far and done so well they should now subdue their voices,
lower their eyes, and compose their features. Why hurry?
After centuries of striving, they had by this time got rid of
their husbands for nine or ten hours at a stretch every day.
The Divorce Court had been established, in 1857, without
the help of afternoon tea.

References

GEORGE BORROW, *The Romany Rye*
O. LANCASTER, *The Story of Tea*
AGNES REPPLIER, *To Think of Tea!*
MADAME DE SÉVIGNÉ, Lettres
THE TEA CENTRE, Sundry publications
HORACE WALPOLE, Letters

VII. Mitigations of Domesticity

THE evidence of the two preceding chapters has confirmed what the reader doubtless knew already—that for the first twenty or thirty years of Victoria's reign Home became a banner, something to be held aloft and pressed forward. It showed where a man had got to, and he clung to it and waved it until the day came when he could exchange it for a bigger and better one. Moreover, the example of the Court, the exhaustion and hunger of lunchless breadwinners, combined to produce long, slow, replete evenings, fretted only by the social rivalries of the ladies and the recurrent compulsion to show, or be shown, an epergne.

An analysis of various works of reference yields statistical proof of the growth of domesticity. Of the more famous clubs of London, about twenty were in existence by 1840. From 1875 clubs began to multiply so rapidly that a commentator, writing in 1911, estimated one-half of the available number as less than thirty years old. But between the years 1840 and 1875 only six clubs of importance were founded.

A good club has always conferred a social cachet, and in the earlier years of the present century a gentleman's visiting card often supplied the reassurance of an 'Arthur's' or a 'Windham' engraved in the corner. Such little advertisements, unobtrusive yet telling, might have been specially designed for the pushful citizens of the eighteen-sixties.

How did they miss them? I think they must have been
blinded by domesticity. The other advantages, though much
prized by the younger sons of good family and limited
means, descendants of the founders of the clubs in which
they passed their days, were less likely to appeal to men who
longed to be mistaken for bankers. Since they always dined
at home or at friends' homes, they were not interested in the
prices of meals and, in any case, would have been nervous of
showing their interest; the attractions of the club dinner
were therefore lost on them. Nevertheless, during the first
fifty or sixty years of the century the cost of meals at the best
of the slowly disappearing coffee-houses and the slowly
appearing hotels and restaurants was astonishingly high, and
throughout this period it was possible to dine at a club for
one-fourth or one-fifth of the price, including the customary
half-pint of wine.[1] Afterwards, too, the member could
smoke, if he pleased, though not nearly so comfortably or so
soon as might be supposed. At White's, cigars were first
allowed in 1845, or 152 years after the club's foundation;
and when, in 1866, a motion was tabled to extend this
licence to the drawing-room, it was defeated by such a
gathering of old members as had never before been seen.
One disgusted smoker swore that, after voting, they re-

[1] Prices varied considerably from club to club and from decade to
decade. In 1828 the select Brooks's served, apparently, two dinners,
one at 10s. 6d. and one at 8s., with an 11 o'clock supper at 6s. In
1834 dinner at the Athenæum cost 3s. 6d., by 1845 that had become
the usual price at most clubs, although, as we have seen, the Duke of
Wellington was satisfied with the joint and half a pint of wine for
two shillings at the United Services. In 1866 the Athenæum served
soup, fish, and entrée for 3s.; a similar meal at the Conservative was
4s. At some clubs, like the Reform, an alternative dinner, 'more complete', cost 7s. or 10s.

entered the waiting hearses and were driven back whence they came.

Much later still, clubs which nowadays reserve at most one room for non-smokers made similar arrangements for smokers. Until 1900 or thereabouts, members of the Athenæum had to troop down to an underground apartment before lighting the noxious weed.

But, as all the evidence in this chapter is designed to show, in or about the year 1875 domesticity began to crack, and then to crack up. In the 1882 edition of the younger Dickens's *Dictionary of London* the clubs of London are listed. Many of them do not affect our immediate argument, but even when the card clubs, the athletic and Old Boys' associations are deducted, what remains suggests, and not by its length alone, that many people had had enough of home life. Already there were two clubs, the New Berners and the Somerville, for ladies only; at three others both ladies and gentlemen were eligible for membership; and at a few more —not the most renowned—ladies were admitted as visitors.

When, in the summer of 1848, the eldest and the youngest Miss Brontë decided that it was time to visit Messrs. Smith and Elder and to demonstrate to the gravelled publisher that they were women, that they were young women, that they were two young women separate from one another and from their sister Ellis, they stopped at the Chapter Coffee House in Paternoster Row. Already most of London's countless coffee-houses were going or gone (not quite countless, presumably, but in the comparatively small city of the early eighteenth century their number was estimated at

2,000), and being replaced rapidly by public houses and slowly by hotels. The Chapter House, a famous hostelry, was not pulled down till 1887, but in the guide-book of 1882 there is no mention of it. Coffee public houses, coffee-palaces, coffee-publics, coffee-taverns are all identified; the term coffee-house never occurs, and we are left reflecting that historic survivals and links with the past are for the confused, the uncertain, the lost ages. Young Dickens belonged to a generation confident of progress, its footsteps rang out on the right road, only an awkward squad of thinkers marring the uniformity. For flourishing concerns of every sort he has his label and his pin. His silence is the coffee-house's monument, and perhaps his.

At many of the new public houses one could get a meal, at others only a snack, but whereas the coffee-houses had been sharply graded all public houses, even the best of them, began to suffer before long from a taint of disreputableness, an infection of the gin-palace. At a time when respectability was classed as almost the first of the virtues, many men did not care and few decent women would dare to be seen in them. For travellers, the residential coffee-houses were replaced by, or reconditioned into, hotels. When, in 1879, Anderton's Hotel arose in Fleet Street, it was a rebuilt version of Anderton's Coffee House which had been, in its turn, a rebuilt version of the Horn on the Hoop, a fourteenth-century tavern and a rival of the Mermaid.

Anderton's was far from being the first hotel to open. At Euston and other railway termini there had been hotels for forty years or more. But, as a stimulus to the business, nothing stands comparison with the Great Exhibition. When it opened, many foreign visitors found accommodation no more luxurious than the White Bear seems likely (from T. H. Shepherd's drawing) to have offered. Before twenty years were up, huge stone hives—some of them have survived to our day—were rising on the Embankment and through the West End. By 1860 there were numerous hotels, for business men, in Holborn and between the Strand and the river, and at varying dates family hotels began to thicken in the Bond Street area and the Buckingham Palace Road. Other early arrivals were the Alexandra in Knightsbridge (the way to Kensington was losing its semi-countrified character), the Langham in Portland Place, Norris's in Addison Road, and, most spectacular of all, the immense Grand Hotel dominating Trafalgar Square. But except for the hotel which we now know as Claridge's, specializing almost from the first in princes, ambassadors, and millionaires, all these establishments were of a utilitarian nature, wholesale lodgings rather than centres of social entertainment. The terms were inclusive, the clients were expected to be punctual and present at meals. These hotels, moreover, built between the years 1850 and 1880, felt no great urge to complicate their menus. Their clients were accustomed to eat where they slept; at home or away, they had little choice in the matter; they had lost or been bullied out of their fathers' love of eating *à la carte* and meekly accepted the table d'hôte.

But by 1880 there were, as already reported, signs of a slight restlessness under routine, the first faint stirrings of a weariness of home. People coming back from holidays in Paris or Brussels brought stories of hotels and restaurants such as London could not show; they complained, they asked why, and their friends were by now ready to listen sympathetically. The results, if not revolutionary, began to be discernible, and by 1882 five or six hotels could be named where 'strangers (even if not staying in the house) can also dine in the coffee-rooms or at the table d'hôte dinners'. In each case, 6 o'clock is the hour given. Presumably theatre-goers formed a good proportion of these strangers but, if so, they cannot have dawdled over the meal. 'A dinner of six courses' was the common advertisement.

Restaurants, under whatever name, had long been plenti-ful in the City. (When the century was already in its last quarter, a visitor to the Royal Exchange could still draw the old distinction and tell of '500 people dining, without count-ing those lunching at the Bar'.) There were also old restau-rants, like Rule's and Simpson's, a little west of Temple Bar. But in fashionable London there were very few restaurants, in the continental sense of that word, until half-way through the century, and their advance, when they came, was significantly timid. Verrey's was perhaps the first. M. Verrey, a Swiss, opened his confectioner's shop in 1825. In addition to a light hand with pastry he possessed a very pretty daughter, and what with one thing and another his business flourished, and even developed: he introduced small tables at which ladies, exhausted by shopping, could rest and consume an ice or a cup of chocolate in the middle of the morning. But he did not go farther. It was his successor, M. Krehl, who turned restaurateur, in 1850 or soon after. In 1863 Gatti's and the Café Royal opened, in 1871 Pagani's, and in 1876 the Monico. It is true that for years

Soho had been spotted with small restaurants, yet the
respectful distance observed by the first large establishments
—intervals of twelve years, eight years, five years—suggests
very cogently that the business was no gold-mine and filled
no long-felt want. In the common practice of including a
grill-room and a restaurant under one roof, some commentators have seen signs of the continued coexistence of the old
devotees of the tavern and the chop-house beside a new,
Frenchified public. It may once have been so; but, though
the two terms have persisted, their implications have dimin-
ished, the modern grill-room, even when there was meat to
grill and coal to grill it on, being often no more than the *à la
carte* department of the (table d'hôte) restaurant.

George Augustus Sala, writing just as the restaurant era
had tentatively opened, was convinced that visitors to London would be enraptured with the food. Twenty-two years
later, young Dickens could do no more than beg them to
believe that things were getting better. The difference may
have been merely one of temperament and standard, or we
may suppose that, with the death or retirement of those
master-cooks who had fled from Paris in 1848, with second-
rate French cooking replacing good English cooking, the
public of 1880 was suffering from the worst of both worlds.
Dickens's list of recommended restaurants, inclusive rather
than exclusive though it seems to be, is not long. It is hard to
believe that some of the *cuisines* he is driven to praise—
Crosby Hall, for instance, or the Royal Aquarium—may
not have left the continental tourists vaguely disappointed.

When luncheon was advertised, and this was seldom, no
details were given. All the honours were still for dinner. 'A

good bedroom, Breakfast of Hot and Cold Meats, Luncheon, a Dinner of Six Courses, and Tea and Coffee in the evening, at a fixed charge of 7s. 6d. per day' was announced by the Caledonian Hotel in Adelphi Terrace. Another hotel in a similar advertisement murmurs, in an aside, that the table d'hôte dinner, usually served at 4 p.m., is at 2 p.m. on Sundays. At the Holborn Restaurant luncheons were obtainable 'from daily bill of fare', but dinners 'at separate tables' are specified as 'soups; two kinds of fish; entrées; joints; sweets; ices; cheese, in variety; salad, &c.', with the added assurance that 'a Selection of Instrumental Music of a refined character performed by a complete Orchestra' is included in the 3s. 6d. charged. At the Criterion and many .other places one could dine as cheaply as at the Holborn, but there were new, smart restaurants, like the Bristol in Burlington Gardens, where the price was as high as 7s. 6d. or half a guinea. At all hotels and restaurants, dinner was served much earlier than in the clients' own homes. The almost invariable hours were 5.30 to 8. In conjecture one must lean again, rather heavily, on the theatre public; one may also imagine an occasional famished business man who, off-colour at breakfast and summoned by the chairman to a biscuit lunch, was ready for dinner long before 5.30. The cocktail party or bar, with its olives, its cheese straws, and its reviving little drinks would have been the very thing for him; it was the invention of a generation which, having had lunch and tea, was more concerned with stimulating than satisfying the appetite.

The first restaurants, then, arriving a little early, were given a hesitating welcome by a home-bound age; and indeed a woman who was raising a numerous family and running a large house for an ambitious husband had little time for relaxation and less opportunity for change. If she went to a restaurant her presence would not excite comment, but she would find herself in a very small minority and, if spoken to by acquaintances, would probably offer an explanation—the visit of the sweep, the orphaning of the cook, or the missing of a train. Even when domesticity was growing rather old, the restaurant habit was still very young. But after the Jubilee the opening of new premises, the recruitment of cooks and waiters, the stocking of cellars and the provision of little tables could hardly keep pace with the demand. A meal at a restaurant was an exciting novelty for a woman, a faint sensation of raffishness adding to the thrill. Husbands were prepared to show their wives what these new places were like, but not to make a habit of it. An old lady whose husband was accustomed to take her to dine once a week at the new Savoy Hotel (opened 1889) has assured me that their close friendship with a playwright was a useful defence of their conduct. It was bohemian—not disreputable, of course, but too far from the standard of domesticity still prevailing in 1890.

Very slight familiarity with the early recurrent editions of Mrs. Beeton's work makes it clear that, even on quiet nights, dinner must have lasted a long time and been succeeded by a lethargy not willingly disturbed. Card parties, theatres, concerts, and other active means of passing the evening entailed an unwelcome, an ever more often avoided, effort. In such an era—the sixties and seventies—the drama inevitably sank to the lowest level, so that the stuffy plays of T. W. Robertson came as a breath of ozone, or as a chilly draught, 'absurdly realistic'. Even promoters, always the most sanguine of men, lost hope. Managers first altered the hours of performance and then, such was their plight, re-revealed them in print. They went further and blurted out that other mystery, the box-office hours; these were from 10 in the morning till 5 in the afternoon. Wasted cunning! Thirty domesticated years passed without a single theatre being built. Then, in 1869, came the Globe; three more joined it in 1870; the Criterion does credit to 1874; during the last two decades of the century at least two dozen new theatres arose.

In their oblique but trustworthy fashion the advertisement columns of *The Times* relate the same story. At the peak of the season in 1865, on 3 June, twelve theatres were trying to attract the public. On the same day in 1880 the number had risen to eighteen. By 3 June 1890 twenty-one theatres were paying for an insertion. Moreover, in the course of this quarter of a century the opening hour had moved, on an average, ninety minutes. One constant feature throughout the period was the curtain-raiser, almost as usual in 1890 as in 1865, and always a source of confusion in estimating the true hour of opening. But whereas in 1865 it often followed the principal play, serving as a curtain-dropper rather than a curtain-raiser and allowing people to get away early, in 1890 it always came first and was valued as a cover for late arrivals. It continued the work of the contortionists and ballad-singers outside the theatre and kept the cheaper seats amused while the stalls and boxes finished their dinners. They had to dine fairly substantially because the gentlemen who paid for the seats had had no lunch to speak of, but they were prepared, for one night only, to cut it a little short if the managers showed an equal willingness to meet them. In this way an honourable compromise had been arrived at, and a far-reaching one; for it resulted in the number of theatres being doubled, the profession of playwright re-established, the players (what was left of them) rescued, revived, and rehearsed, and City gentlemen reminded, on leaving home, that it was only a light dinner. Some of those gentlemen began to absent themselves from Birch's and to slink into chop-houses, just as if they were senior clerks.

The attractions of the dining-room and drawing-room were slightly less damaging to musicians, since there are always and everywhere people for whom music is a positive necessity, a craving which nothing, certainly no mere phase of domesticity, can numb. At Her Majesty's Theatre (then Her Majesty's Opera House) opera was usually given throughout the year, even the darkest years of the period; at Covent Garden, Italian opera was staged during the Season, after the winter pantomimes and before the autumn Promenade Concerts; and though prices were high and confusing to the issue, bringing in considerations of social advancement, these enterprises cannot be ignored. A still healthier sign was the foundation of the Guildhall and Trinity Schools and the Royal College of Music. But these educational centres date from the years surrounding 1880; when Covent Garden Opera House abandoned its policy of concerts with occasional performances of operas by Balfe and Benedict, when it ventured on 'Royal Italian Opera', it failed; and Her Majesty's, after being hired in 1875 for the revivalist meetings of Moody and Sankey, did not reach its operatic peak till a few years later.

If we are looking for evidence that Belgravia and Port-man Square were willing to leave their comfortable chairs for anything less sensational than a Joachim or a Pauline Lucca, we find ourselves on still shakier ground. The younger Dickens's claim ('we may take it now as an ac-cepted fact that in few other countries does music enter more universally into the lives of the people') has a familiar ring, yet it can seldom have been made with less justification. The Hanover Square Rooms and two other concert halls had recently closed their doors; there was occasionally a performance by a choral society at the Albert Hall, 'but occurrences in connection with this ill-fated building are not of much general importance'; the Eyre Arms and the Horns at Kennington were recommended as suitable for charitable purposes; but for the public at large the alter-natives were the inaccessible Crystal Palace, odd seasons at Covent Garden, and the new St. James's Hall. This, it is true, was a considerable affair. It stood on the site now occu-pied by the Piccadilly Hotel, and contained two halls, a large and a small. A popular restaurant, lectures and the Moore and Burgess Minstrels, recitals and concerts, all helped to create an atmosphere of activity and even to anticipate our notions of an Art Centre. Like the later Queen's Hall, it was the headquarters of musical London.

What were the concerts? One must go to some trouble to

find out, for the day was far distant, if it has yet fully dawned, when musical arrangements were plainly and conveniently stated in the newspapers. In 1865 one had to wade through two columns of mixed advertisements in *The Times*, many of them inserted by publishers (at such times and places 'Mr. Whiffin will sing *Thou Wilt Be True*') and many of them dealing with music-hall performances, instrument-makers' addresses, and other matters not strictly concerned with the programmes. By 1885 the confusion was worse still. The two columns had swollen to three and a half, and to the vaguely musical items were added the vaguely artistic. The following is a fair sample of the hundreds of insertions and of the order in which they were arranged: an Exhibition of International Inventions, engravings, picture shows, poetry recitals, a Handel Festival at the Crystal Palace, Mr. S. E. Waller's new painting '*Twixt Love and Duty* at the St. James's Gallery, Fancy Dress balls, Mme Mary Cummings will sing *A Face in the Crowd*, demonstration of mesmerism, Maskelyne and Cooke at the Egyptian Hall, a Wagner concert conducted by Herr Richter, table d'hôte at 5 at the Crystal Palace, Mr. and Mrs. German Reed's free dates. The situation had clearly passed out of control, and by 1890 the announcements were presented in something like order and something like classification. The names of new, small concert halls were beginning to appear, but though we find mention of recitals by performers of world-wide repute, the ballad concert still predominated; it continued for many more years to be the surest method of filling a hall. Yet if, once more, we can trace a degradation of taste to the preceding and domesticated years, we can see also that there was still a public. Even in those drawing-rooms *morceaux* had gone on being played on pianos, and amateur tenors, throttled by food and high collars, had not ceased to render songs by Frederic Clay and J. L. Hatton. It all added up, perhaps, to something, if not much.

While Society was ignoring the theatre and, unless the seats were expensive and evening dress compulsory, getting its music at home, humbler people dining earlier and more briefly and inhabiting less comfortable houses clung to the belief that it was fun to have an evening out. Accustomed from childhood to confuse domesticity with congestion, they liked to escape from pokiness to grandeur; and whereas, in thirty years, not one theatre was built, six of London's largest music-halls were erected in seven years, between 1857 and 1864. The songs and choruses of the taverns were continued and elaborated in the earliest public houses; there was thus an existing audience for Variety, and more and more publicans found it profitable to buy an adjoining building, improvise stages and curtains, and engage turns. The performances would run from six to midnight or later, with occasional reminders from the Chairman that, unless more drinks were ordered and more victuals consumed, the artistes could no longer be adequately remunerated and the entertainment must be concluded. Some of these next-door premises, these adjuncts to bars, turned eventually into established music-halls, the Middlesex and the Canterbury both beginning in that manner; others failed to withstand the competition of the great palaces of Variety which presently arose; but there was a time, in the seventies and eighties, when dancers and singers, ventriloquists and conjurors, jugglers and performing animals, comics and campanologists, acrobats and sword-swallowers, mimics and midgets, Queens of Equilibrium and boneless wonders had somehow to be found for 500 audiences every night. The evenings of the common man were filled with music and laughter, with noise and change. The entertainments were virile, the patter and songs of the comediennes as masculine and muscular as those of the comedians. The audience, too, was predominantly male; in short, what with the drinks and smoke, the bars and waiters, the fun and jokes, nothing could have been less like home; and, for that very reason, there were always a few broadminded wives and sweethearts who contrived to get themselves taken along.

Since the patrons of Variety usually occupied modest positions in the social and economic systems and, when the lights were at last turned out, had often some distance to go, it is at first sight surprising to find that the great Music Halls tended to open later than the theatres. But in spite of a series of Acts which had been, for forty or fifty years, setting limits to the customers' convenience and improving the lot of the shop-assistants, long hours were still worked in offices and stores. The employer might reach home at 6, he left his staff closing down or tidying up for another hour or more. If the opening hours of all entertainments were later, there was no corresponding curtailment of programmes; on the contrary, they went on competing in generosity.

Yet all the early-closing Acts in the world cannot drive everyone to bed. In all ages and cities and ranks of life there are people who dislike going home—the bohemians, the idle bachelors, the dissolute, the merely lonely. There had always been plenty of oyster bars and other supper resorts, respectable enough places where, though real ladies would not, unreal ones could not enter, and an assembly of middle-aged gentlemen sat at long, wooden tables, raising their voices and glasses in chorus. One of the most popular— Evans's Hotel and Supper Rooms, in Covent Garden—has a double claim to our attention for, though something bigger and better than the public houses which were to copy it, it offered its patrons a stage and entertainers, thereby earning for itself the title of the first of the music-halls. But now there were springing up new, exciting, gallant establishments like Romano's and the Criterion, and rowdier spots like the Café de l'Europe. Even as they arose, the shadow of legislation fell across them. We hear complaints that, soon after midnight, a subtle feeling of illegality and less subtle signs of unrest among the waiters led to the dispersal, or at least the depression, of the company. In such circumstances people leave before they wish, and though many of them may head rather sadly for home, there are— and there were in 1880—others who hold that the best hour of the twenty-four has now arrived. For them and for their custom numerous 'clubs' were formed on lines familiar enough to us but not, or so some of us had believed, to our grandfathers. Free of the restrictions, these places remained open 'until the small hours grew large again. It may be added that the rules of many of these clubs are easy, and their committees kind. Little difficulty need therefore be apprehended in obtaining admission to one or other of these *quasi* taverns.'

The chapter has been a long but not, I hope, an idle digression. It is not yet ended. Here is the day of a young man apprenticed, at the age of twenty, to a solicitor in 1880. He ate one of Mrs. Beeton's best breakfasts at 8.30; lunched off one of those eternal biscuits and glasses of sherry; never thought of afternoon tea, 'a young ladies' fad', unless it came his way as sometimes on a Sunday; and enjoyed one of Mrs. Beeton's minor but still considerable dinners at 7.30 or 7.45. Being an apprentice, he played football on Saturday afternoons; the other clerks went on working.

That was the day's shape for every man[1] who was Something—professional or commercial—in the City, and it had a long innings, forty years or more, enduring into the new century and even as late as the first Great War. There may be a few men following it still; every City gentleman who has now celebrated his seventieth birthday knew it once upon a time. With its almost unsupported span of eleven hours between breakfast and dinner, the day was passed in a commercial monastery, where the rigorous and rather bleak routine was as far from what preceded it as from what was to follow. It lacked altogether the leisure and high spirits of the Regency, it was unrelieved by the frivolous noises of our day, the crockery, the giggles, the wooden heels. It was the accompaniment, the setting, of a vast prosperity; but when, in the evening, men escaped from its strain, their exhaustion

---

[1] There are always the few exceptions. In Anstey's *Vice Versa*, published in the same year as Dickens's *Dictionary* (1882), Mr. Bultitude, a Colonial Produce merchant of Mincing Lane and the reluctant hero of this famous novel, went to his club for a hot lunch. But his time-table, as revealed in the opening chapters, is so confused and improbable that I think we may ignore it.

was apt to cramp the family circle to which they turned for relaxation, putting it in a state of defence, closing it against them. The age was fortunate but not always happy.

If the pattern of the business day becomes distinct, my overlaying design compels me at once to disturb it with sundry qualifications, some of them contradicting what has just been said. The young gentleman mentioned above, now a very old gentleman, had an uncle who in 1880 was still dining at 6 and having tea, cake, and sandwiches at 9, and there were plenty like him everywhere and for some time to come. 'My grandmother', writes a Frenchman, 'who was 89 when she died in 1908 had her *petit déjeûner* on waking, her *déjeûner* at 11 a.m., and her *souper* (we called it her *dîner* but she called it her *souper*) at six. It was only after years of wrangling with my father that she finally had the evening meal delayed to 7.30 when, on Sundays, she had the whole family round her table.'

That English uncle, that French grandmother were a little old fashioned, but neither would have been considered eccentric in the eighties, when popular restaurants in the City of London still served two dinners, one at 1 o'clock and the other at 4, with eleven kinds of fish and a selection of joints.

Something—I am not sure what—on some unidentifiable date—perhaps about 1870—had happened. No doubt it was not so sudden as to impress itself upon the notice of people living at that time, and even now it is difficult to describe it more precisely than as a certain loosening, and lightening, and splitting up; and among possible causes the choice is embarrassingly wide, from ever-mounting wealth to the exotic influence of FitzGerald and Swinburne, from the defeat of our age-long enemies at Sedan to the late Georgian traits exhibited by the Heir to the Throne. All or none of these may have played their part, or the ladies may simply have been breaking out again. *Reculées* for years, they may well have thought it was once more time to *sauter*, to regain a control they had somehow lost. It may have all begun with a hostess preparing herself for the reception of eighteen guests and one of those interminable dinners, a woman with hardly any little pots and boxes, with nothing but a powder-puff, scrutinizing her exhausted face in a mirror and calling through the dressing-room door to demand why ten kinds of fish had to be offered rather than nine or even eight, and if anybody would be seriously affronted by a choice of five hot joints in place of six, or six sweets instead of seven.

Whatever it sprang from, even if the natives were unaware of it, this loosening-up process was at work; and a newly arrived, non-English, and remarkably sensitive intelligence, unencumbered by memory and habit and freshly turned upon the scene, 'noted and tasted and assimilated' it immediately. No one can read the first English stories of Henry James without realizing how utterly different they must have been if written only ten years sooner or by a resident author, familiar, close, and not always in focus. In one of the earliest of all he shows us two sisters from Boston staying in 'one of those places just out of Piccadilly', called upon by the usual cosmopolitan fellow countryman, and conducted by him, at 5.30 on a summer evening, to sit for an hour or two on little green chairs in Hyde Park, watching the carriages, the equestrians, and the clothes, identifying the celebrated and the notorious. 'In America', Mrs. Westgate is driven to remark, 'there is no leisure class', and her words, her voice, are a tangle of mixed emotions. The scene at which she gazed had been described by Sala, but as James shows it to her and to us it is almost empty of Sala and full of Anthony Hope; or the year might have been 1779 or the gardens the Bois de Boulogne; or London might have been one of its own Stilton cheeses, emitting a whiff of rottenness which the lady from Massachusetts could not entirely approve but recognized as what she was after, a sign of the real thing. Not for forty or fifty years past would she have got so much for her money.

References

F. ANSTEY, *Vice Versa*
H. C. COLLES, *Grove's Dictionary of Music* (4th ed.)
CHARLES DICKENS, JR., *Dictionary of London* (1882)
M. W. DISHER, *Winkles & Champagne*
HENRY JAMES, JR., *An International Episode* (1879)
WM. KENT, *Encyclopaedia of London*
JAMES LAVER, *Eating Out*
London Society, vol. x
R. NEVILL, *London Clubs*
Unpublished correspondence.

VIII. The Turn of the Century

A DAY may come, if it has not already dawned, when the closing years of Victoria's reign are bathed in a light which, less brilliant than the Elizabethan, rivals the Johnsonian glow. Leaving posterity, however, to select its own raptures, we can ask ourselves if the once derided nineties were not, in fact, one of those 'best times' recurring, at intervals, in the histories of all countries. For such men and women as have provided the matter of this book, life, if lacking some earlier graces, was most agreeably dignified; it was pleasant, it was very comfortable, above all it was sure. The ground beneath the feet had never been firmer, and its firmness had lasted so long that people took it for granted, never doubting that the smooth road was approaching a beautiful and permanent terminus, that they were very nearly There. They were absolutely certain about the next day, they could depend upon the next year, they had no reason for not putting full reliance on the next ten years. From knowing exactly where they were and finding the spot good, they may have become rather self-satisfied and apt to try to improve the foreigner, the poor, and all who were denied their advantages. They suffered from complacency, or made others suffer, and their souls put on weight. The resistance, then, of a handful of Boers came as a shock; the discovery of Little Englanders in their midst upset them no less. But they were happy, enthusiastically if not very exaltedly happy; they were bringing back happiness at the end of an era, the sternest since Cromwell's, during which it had been suspected, disapproved of, and sometimes, from the highest motives, turned out of doors. In the countenances gazing out from their flamboyant photographs we do not find, or so it seems to me, the dedicated look impressed, suitably or unsuitably, on the faces of their mothers, or the burnt out, equally baffled eyes of their descendants. We can call their appearance smug or serene, but not unhappy.

The material comfort of their lives was matched by the mental and spiritual, for the signs of Progress, wherever they looked, were so clear and abundant as to amount to evidence of Divine approbation. To wealth and a deep reservoir of indoor and outdoor servants, to leisure and no shortages, there was added the endless succession of convenient inventions. 'Science' had done much of its best work, its worst was still to come. Its reputation was unsmirched, it was treated as a friend. In beautiful condition, it was rolled round the tongue like the wines matured in their ample cellars. How comforting, indeed, those first sips must have been, how rosy! Fate has compelled us to drink a little deeper in the glass. Like Leontes, we have seen the spider.

Early morning

In all households it was by now customary to fortify the occupants of the best bedrooms with a cup of tea before rising. The spread of the week-end habit brought with it a more complicated ritual and this, of course, especially affected the staff. A kitchen-maid might have to be down by 4.30 a.m. to prepare the *brioches* for the main breakfast table and for the trays with which smart and travelled ladies were beginning to be served in bed. Cook herself was expected to be down not later than 6.45, and to find the housemaids busy on the hall, the staircases, and reception rooms. If, as sometimes happened, the back stairs did not mount to the maids' quarters but stopped halfway up the house, there was a certain amount of dark and early rustling and tiptoeing past the bedrooms of the gentry who thus might or might not be awake when, at an agreed moment between 7.45 and 8.15, there came a knock on the door. The snug acknowledgement was rarely effective; almost always a short pause preceded a second knock, after which a maid entered carrying a tray with tea and bread and butter or, disappointingly, a Marie biscuit. In summer she placed the tray beside the bed and then pulled the curtains; in winter, she might leave the tray outside until she had pulled the curtains and could see where she was going. If the morning was very dark, she might light a candle on the mantelpiece. She was followed by a smaller, younger, rather scared maid with an ash-bin, paper, firing wood, blacking, brushes, and a pair of gloves, who, after re-laying the fire, lit it. Unless she was very expert the clattering of her implements was disturbing, but the guest could put his head beneath the clothes so long as he did not go to sleep again before the next stage. The maid, having removed her pots and pans, brushes and gloves, now spread a waterproof mat on the carpet, dragged a hip-bath on to it, placed the bath towel on a chair near the fire, and asked when she should bring the hot water. In London or the country she carried this, later, from the basement to the second or third floor in huge cans.

Establishments varied, of course, in size and splendour, and it might happen that hardly had the bachelor, sipping his first cup of tea, begun to regain spirituality, to feel his soul seeping back from its nocturnal ebbing, than another knock, another door-opening, introduced a footman with a folded suit over his arm and a pair of shoes, or rather boots, in his hand. His brief weather report was a prelude to discussion of apparel suited to the temperature and pleasing to the eye, after which he laid out the approved garments, hid the evening shirt in merciful obscurity and removed, for loving treatment, the dress clothes.

A gifted and conscientious footman provided (his death is assumed) endless little attentions. I remember one who, while omitting nothing, always sent me home with my suitcase half-empty, though it had been bursting when I came. I remember another who took out, ironed, and reinserted the laces of my shoes.

Except in the rooms of the children and of young gentlemen still at the University, fires were usual. The guest rose —for he did, eventually, rise—to a well-intentioned if still rather adolescent fire, found it blazing when he dressed for dinner and glowing when he went to bed. In novel after novel of the period, the day ends with the hero standing thoughtfully by the mantelpiece, his face lit from below, or with the heroine, in a becoming wrap and an armchair, prodding the coals impatiently and wondering just what a gentleman had meant.

Breakfast

In the London homes of men of affairs breakfast was at

8 or 8.30, and punctuality, the salient quality of the Victorian age, was still manifest. If daughters or young sons wished to ride in the Row, they were expected to be back in time or else to postpone their exercise till after breakfast. Prayers often preceded the meal, all members of the household being present except, perhaps, a French lady's maid or an Irish girl in the kitchen. The domestics were paraded in the hall, and with Cook in front and the butler at the rear entered the dining-room in single file. A horse-shoe of chairs, with a hymn-book on the seat, awaited them. Already accommodated on a smaller horse-shoe, its back to the windows, the Family watched the procession, noting or perhaps failing to note, among subterranean juniors never glimpsed save at this hour, a new face.

There is little fresh to be said about the meal itself. More and more it had developed a character and dishes of its own. Of the chops and cold meats of an earlier generation nothing remained but an occasional cold partridge in autumn and winter. Up to 1920 and even 1930 one could still meet old gentlemen who, in their youth, had begun a hunting day with a steak and a pint of claret, but even if they were still riding out they had long grown accustomed to nothing more sustaining than kedgeree or a fried slip with buttered eggs and bacon to follow, nothing more nerving than coffee. A large silver tea urn or kettle remained part of the table's furniture. The mistress peeped from, or on difficult mornings hid, behind it.

A son might be setting out from home[1] at 9 o'clock or

[1] There were still a few professional men—lawyers, architects, publishers, and so on—living above their offices, but by the end of the

earlier, his father was known to be an hour behind him. The
ever-increasing efficiency of the postal services, the ever-
increasing use of the typewriter, the ever-increasing multiplication of charities produced an ever-increasing pile of
letters beside the plate at the end of the table. It was sometimes 10 or 10.15—just when Evelina would have been
sitting down to breakfast—before the harassed man could
burst, with a roar, from his 'library'. Woe betide the wife,
child, coachman or other domestic who then tried to catch
and question him on his way to the front door, or who was
not there waiting to receive his shouted instructions!

Luncheon

When the nineties opened, the usual hour for lunch was
1 o'clock. But although guests were beginning to be more
frequent, I think that, at this time, they were apt to be
relatives rather than friends. The family spirit was still
strong; the old French lady's Sunday evening gatherings,
mentioned in the last chapter, were paralleled all over London by Sunday luncheons, delayed till 2 o'clock (the staff had
been depleted by attendance at church where sermons, if not
what they used to be, were yet much longer than they are
today), competed for by rival grandparents, and submitted
to, not without some grumblings, by the whole clan. At the
close of the decade, or at the beginning of the next, the
luncheon hour can be observed moving, in the old sweet
way, clockwise. Luncheon parties were becoming more
fashionable and frequent, the invitations often mentioning

Edwardian decade they had practically all been driven, by the telephone, to separate their residence and their place of business.

1.45 for a meal which was prone to be served at 2. No hostess hoped to achieve the dinner-time alternation of the sexes, but with the help of retired military and naval officers, the clergy, and one or two young gentlemen who 'wrote' or were hoping for an interview with Mr. George Alexander, the party acquired a little masculine dilution. These blameless gentlemen occupied a curious position in the family conscience. Useful in the middle of the day, they were not willingly referred to in the evening when, even after a good dinner, the Head of the House could easily be irritated by a picture of men lunching substantially.

But whereas Miss Austen and Miss Edgeworth had pounced upon luncheon when it was a novelty, the story-tellers of the nineties are strangely indifferent to its renewed blossoming. They occasionally mention it, they never make much of it, or as much as we might expect. Perhaps the meal made a sudden advance in sociability in or about the year 1900. It is, in fact, in a story written in 1903 that I have found the first reference to a luncheon party which seems to me, by modern standards, to be just, if indefinably, right. But by then the pile of evidence is so vast that no one can get to the end of it, and there may well be a thousand earlier and no less authentic descriptions—casual, glancing, assured of the reader's easy comprehension—of a recognized thing.

Afternoon tea

Those same novelists had no such hesitation here. In big houses tea was by now a formal affair, with cake-stands, hot dishes, and small trays borne to and fro by footmen who remained in attendance throughout the meal. Five o'clock was a fashionable hour, or even later; in one of Mrs. Humphry Ward's stories week-end guests, arriving at about 5.45, found tea prepared for them in the red drawing-room and their hostess 'clad by Annette, the maid, in a frock of state', ready to serve and share it. When there was company, ladies dressed for tea before dressing for dinner. When the tea party was regular and larger, when a lady announced that she would be found At Home every third Wednesday, she might engage professional musicians, and her guests would certainly wear their most elaborate *toilettes*. When there was no company, or none to speak of, the tea gown came out.

But there is plenty of evidence that the meal's intimate possibilities were at length being appreciated. Gossipy teas, teas for two, teas from which men were excluded, easy confidential teas—they all begin to make their frequent appearances, turning up in every other chapter and unconsciously revealing enjoyment of a new pleasure. They all consisted of very thin bread and butter, with either a Madeira, Seed, or Dundee cake; a slightly superior form included cucumber sandwiches in summer and buttered toast or Sally Lunns in winter. Everybody was discovering afternoon tea. Some people were glad, for one reason or another, to take it away from home. The first A.B.C. shop had opened in 1880; it was at London Bridge where, northward in the morning and southward at night, pioneer typists were crossing the frontiers of a world unprepared for them. When the first Lyons followed, in 1894, it was, significantly, in Piccadilly.

Dinner

The usual hour begins to bear a very familiar look—7.30 to 7.45 on quiet evenings, 7.45 for 8 for a party. Visiting an old English lady who, though living alone, dined always at 8, one of Henry James's young Americans remarks with surprise that 'she appeared to keep these immense hours'; and it is true that slightly festive suggestions garlanded the clock at 8. It was the hour of hospitality rather than of comfort, and at the mention of it any man, unless otherwise instructed, brought out his tail coat[1] while his wife went through her long gloves. A dinner-party called for great preparation, and in normal households, where the mistress could not leave the arrangements to a housekeeper but had to do much of the work herself, it was not unusual to restrict such functions to two a month, held on successive nights.

Though Mrs. Beeton might have thought it *mesquin*, the meal was still considerable. For the family alone, the menu card, in the handwriting of the butler or the head parlour-maid, showed five courses; it almost had to, for there, at the end of the table, was that famished man who, unsatisfied by soup, fish, entrée, and sweet, might well want a second helping of the joint. On company nights, seven courses were the thing. The set and balanced table, with 'removes' and other complications, had quite gone, and the service was what we now understand, or what had once been called, *à la Russe*. Further traces of informality were affecting, too, the imposing procession from drawing-room to dining-room. Though the seniors were still scrupulously paired a hostess

[1] Hitherto, he had had no choice. The dinner-jacket seems to have remained obstinately uninvented till 1898.

might, in smiling but not unstudied fellowship, bid the younger guests sort themselves. This meant that they were free to choose, not to straggle. For every white glove there had to be a black elbow.

After dinner servants occasionally were seen going round the company with cups of tea, but as the turn of the century drew near the practice became old fashioned. More commonly the hostess, having ushered out the ladies, found coffee in the drawing-room, whence rather cold cups reached, in due course, the dining-room. When the time came for the gentlemen to join them, there was apt to be a moment of hesitation, of exchanged glances, of half-gestures. The host was being given his chance to say 'Liberty Hall!' If he did not, cigars and those slightly un-English, slightly doubt-instilling cigarettes were pressed into peach skins or dropped into finger-bowls. Such niceness has not yet entirely gone, but it is very rare today. It was common till 1914.

In the drawing-room, with the company reassembled, there might be conversation or cards, but the chances continued to be in favour of music. The little world bordered by Queen's Gate and Knightsbridge, by Eaton and Montagu Squares, was as full as ever of baritones striving to be tenors, of ladies who liked to be described as *mezzos*, and it was good manners for the hostess to ask if they had brought their music with them and, anxiety on the point being dispelled, for the guests to murmur delightedly. The amateur accompanist was unfortunate indeed if he found himself confronted with an unfamiliar score. The difficulty was, rather, to avoid clashings among candidates who specialized, one and all, in interpreting the work of Guy d'Hardelot and Teresa del Riego.

Sometimes a professional entertainer was provided, generally in the form of a shy girl or perspiring youth from one of the musical conservatoires who, besides helping the evening to pass, was comfortingly understood to be, in turn, 'helped' by the ordeal; a tactful hostess would be careful to see that the young person was an instrumentalist, not a vocalist. A rather special occasion, with a novel importation, forms the subject of one of my own recollections of the period. The Sunday gatherings at my grandmother's mounted, annually, to the peak of her Christmas dinner. With the help of my aunts and uncles and cousins, of second cousins and a few lonely bachelors and spinsters, she managed to collect a company approximating to Mrs. Beeton's favourite number of eighteen; the table-centre was a mountain range of crackers surrounded by a rivulet of silver *bonbonnières*; the servants, regular and rosy, with their reinforcements, white and anxious, rushed and collided and muttered; the inevitable spread, like red carpet for Royalty, unrolled. There was goose as well as turkey, roast beef as well as poultry; after the pudding the mince pies, no mere consorts, succeeded on clean plates to the vacant throne.

My grandmother, though doubtless pleased to do what was expected of her, never claimed, I imagine, to have done more. But on the occasion I have in mind there was a light of pride in her eyes. Her Christmas dinners, however normal, were not calculated to put any son-in-law in good voice; some years had passed since *Songs of Araby* had been even attempted, and she must have decided that the time had come when the threat of it might, without offence, be ignored. She announced a surprise. When, urgently summoned from the dining-room, we made our way upstairs, the grown-ups openly regretting their curtailed, and self-supplied, cigars, we children pounding on ahead, munching crystallized ginger and wondering if there could possibly be more presents, we found in the drawing-room a strange man with a strange box. We stopped silent on the threshold. My grandmother came forward. The gentleman, she explained, was from Whiteley's, and his box was that wonder of the age, that novelty we had heard of but never seen, a gramophone. I gazed at him as if he were the inventor; he had a black moustache, and he bowed twice, and then, without a word, began his mystic rites. For an hour his records wheezed, hissed, and crackled, the faint, faraway, muffled voices singing familiar, just recognizable songs; and we sat and listened and marvelled. During the last few years other grandmothers have delighted other grandchildren with their first glimpse of television, but not, surely, with comparable effect. The parents as well as the children have had, all their lives, the cinema to prepare them for this revelation. We barely had had the rumoured phonograph, superseded before attaining perfection or popularity, obsolete almost at the moment of marketing.

It will be seen that the hostess had, in one way or another, to plan her big evenings, and they were apt to be lengthier than they are now. We can read in the novels of the day of people being invited to 'drop in' on no very exceptional gathering and arriving, without qualms, at 11.30. But however protracted the talk or the music, there is never a hint of supper or even sandwiches. Except after theatres and concerts they had, of course, been out of fashion for half a century; they would have been, in Mrs. Beeton's eyes, an insult. The decay of domesticity, with its concomitant variations of the course of the evening, might have let them in again but, in the event, the late Victorian and early Edwardian dinner proved equal to holding them at bay.

Smoking

Tobacco's slow climb to acceptance has been noted from time to time. Gentlemen were still hesitating to smoke in the presence of ladies, but whereas, in Disraeli's novels, they were restricted to the late hours and the bachelors' wing, they now had a recognized apartment. Three spaced and dated extracts from stories by Henry James will indicate the progress of the campaign.

The first is from *The Liar*, published in 1888. As the ladies, in a 'rustling procession', retire for the night, Colonel Capadose turns to a young man, remarks 'I hope you smoke', and then leaves the room. 'He appeared ten minutes later in the smoking-room, in a brilliant equipment, a suit of crimson foulard covered with little white spots . . . he might have passed for a Venetian of the sixteenth century. . . . All the gentlemen collected at Stayes were not smokers and some of them had gone to bed. Colonel Capadose remarked that there would probably be a smallish muster, they had had such a hard day's work. That was the worst of a hunting house. . . . But most fellows revived under the stimulating influences of the smoking-room, and some of them, in this confidence, would turn up yet. . . . Lyon was alone with Colonel Capadose for some moments before their companions, in varied eccentricities of uniform, straggled in.'

The next is from *The Lesson of the Master*, published three years later. 'The smoking-room at Summersoft was on the scale of the rest of the place; that is it was high and light and commodious, and decorated with such refined old carvings and mouldings that it seemed rather a bower for ladies who should sit at work at fading crewels than a parliament of gentlemen smoking strong cigars. The gentle-men mustered there in considerable force on the Sunday evening ... in bright habiliments.' But not all. Some, now, were 'without a change of dress'.

Ten years later, 1901, in *The Story In It*, a gentleman after tea with two ladies is 'allowed to light' a cigarette.

In the course of a beautiful description of week-ends at Augustus Hare's in 1898 and 1899, Mr. Somerset Maug-ham tells us that his host 'neither smoked himself, nor allowed smoking in the house, so that such of his guests as hankered for the first pipe of the day had to go into the garden, which was pleasant enough in summer when you could sit down with a book, but not so pleasant in winter when you had to seek shelter in the stables'.

In what were then known as Society novels, a Pipe never enters a Mansion, or only in the mouth of a big-game hunter. Schoolmasters, authors, artists, country doctors, men one did not expect to meet there, might be supposed to smoke a pipe; from the Jubilee till the death of Edward VII a pipe played a significant and useful part, with the aid of a violin and a hypodermic syringe, in setting Sherlock Holmes at a distance. In general, however, it was the mark of humble birth or circumstances. By 1905 perhaps (it is hard to be precise) City gentlemen shooting partridges in Suffolk or grouse in Perthshire could be seen linking themselves with the soil by struggling to keep one alight.

The day

The first thing to notice is the gradual change which, from the day when Trade grew respectable, had been coming over breakfast. Evelina had doubted if it could be called a meal. Seventy-five years later the cookery books were prescribing a four-course breakfast for week-days; for another seventy-five years or more, undergraduates were easily disposing of Sunday breakfasts of five courses—porridge, fish, scrambled eggs, sausages and bacon, marmalade—each course accompanied by a round or two of buttered toast and the whole concluded, in the firm belief that the system called for it, with an apple. Though sometimes lacking time for its full relish, plenty of Englishmen came to consider it the best meal of the day. Whereas, then, at the beginning of the nineteenth century, the hours preceding 4 p.m. were, for comfortable people, a mere prelude to the hours which followed it, a very different conception of the day, a new shape, came into existence long before the twentieth.

Both the old conception and the new had unexpected features. When dinner was much the most important, was almost the only meal of the day, every kind of chance or circumstance was allowed to affect its hour, yet the relatively insignificant breakfast remained steady at 10 a.m. Soon after the century was halfway through, breakfast was being served at any time between 7.45 and 9 a.m., according to the position of the house; the variations in the dinner hour seldom exceeded thirty minutes. Dinner, indeed, which had once been the peak of the day's experiences, now tended to mark, instead, the end of the day's labours. It had been an invariable, it was now an exceptional, form of celebration. It had been a natural, it had become an organized, occasion for high spirits.

The simple halves of the day, morning and evening, before and after dinner, had changed for all women and most men into quarters, morning, afternoon, between tea and dinner, and after dinner. Possibly the amount of food eaten at breakfast, luncheon, tea, and dinner added up to as much as, in some cases more than, the quantities consumed in the huge repasts of the Georgians; yet inevitably dinner, as its auxiliaries grew more numerous, lost something of its size and supremacy—it was the President but no longer the King.

Already, in 1900, we are on the threshold of the snack and snippet age. Friends and relatives, to whom an invitation had formerly implied a settling in for five or six weeks, now came from Friday night to Monday morning unless, better still, they came from Saturday morning to Sunday night. With the help of the telephone and, now, the motor-car, people could make quicker contacts, so that the art of letter-writing became an anachronism; they could also make quicker escapes, so that, gaining proficiency in the rapid exchange of news, they were presently filled with dismay by the prospect of an evening of sedate conversation. The three-volume novel, having survived the hazards of 150 years, decided to retire in about 1890; quill pens soon followed it. A lady, after dressing when she got up and dressing again on her return from a canter in the Row, might dress again if she were going out to lunch, dress again for tea and, for a fifth time, for dinner. In her re-emergence from the housekeeper decades, in her new, dazzling, but rather jumpy existence, she could and often did spend three to four hours a day in dressing and undressing; and, exhausted by the elaborate processes, she was apt to seek her bedroom for a further hour, between 6 and 7, when she rested. Let us pay her the tribute of a short pause, watching her as she slowly mounts the stairs and disappears along the landing. Something is disappearing with her, turning her rest into a last rest. Within two decades, reposing ladies were to pass out of fashion; within two more, ladies.

As dinners became later, so did theatres. There were eight-fifteens among their advertisements, but eight-thirty predominated, and there were occasional eight-forty-fives. Everybody, in a pre-cocktail age, could dress, swallow a curtailed but nourishing meal, and reach the theatre punctually, if so inclined. By June 1900 only seven theatres were staging curtain-raisers; by June 1910 the number had dropped to three. Since 1919 recognized playwrights have seldom troubled to contrive short plays unless, like Barrie and Mr. Coward, they find material for three of them to make up an evening's entertainment.

References

ANTHONY HOPE, *The Dolly Dialogues*
HENRY JAMES, *A London Life*

THE TURN OF THE CENTURY

HENRY JAMES. *The Liar*
—— *The Lesson of the Master*
—— *Sir Edmund Orme*
—— *Flickerbridge*
—— *Mrs. Medwin*
—— *The Story In It*
—— *The Beast in the Jungle*
W. SOMERSET MAUGHAM, 'Augustus' (*Cornhill*, No. 981)
MRS. HUMPHRY WARD, *Sir George Tressady*
Unpublished correspondence

IX. To be Continued

PLEASANTLY, rather monotonously, yet not without occasional surprises the story was to proceed on its way —it might have been called a permanent way but for its lack of termini. The landscape was deteriorating, but there were still some old landmarks to be seen. The Sunday delivery of letters in the country, for instance, continued into the third decade of the century. In the following decade there was the startling new tenancy of the three-volume novel, derelict for forty years or more. It is true that it was done up as one volume, but it took just as long to read and was far heavier to hold. Even famous novelists were warned by their publishers that they must master the knack of making three words do the work of one, or nobody would have time to read them.

The return of long books in an age that seemed designed for the short story is, however, merely one more awkward factor in the chronicle—like the reluctance of Victorian men to eat in the middle of the day, or the slowness of their wives to realize the possibilities of afternoon tea. More characteristic features call for our attention. Subject to American and continental influences and their own inherent tendencies, the social and spiritual descendants of Pope's friend, the Countess of Suffolk, had by 1925 decided to breakfast in bed, at 8.15 or thereabouts, off a glass of orange juice, a piece of toast Melba, a cup of coffee unsugared and black, and cigarettes. Their husbands did little better, in fact they often shared the meal—'if it may be called a *meal*'. As a result of this flimsy start to the day, lunch was moving a little against the clock; the 1.30 or 1.45 of the Edwardians was by now 1.15 or even 1. Moreover it had at length firmly established itself with the men, so firmly that, with a client for company and business as an excuse, they occupied more and more tables at the Carlton and the Savoy. It had indeed become for many people the most substantial meal of the day. They might not recognize it as such, they never dreamed of changing its name, yet it was near to displaying the four characteristics of Dinner as laid down by De Quincey. Here they are again, repeated from Chapter IV:

1. That dinner is that meal, no matter when taken, which is the principal meal *i.e.* the meal on which the day's support is thrown.
2. That it is *therefore* the meal of hospitality.
3. That it is the meal (with reference to both Nos. 1 and 2) in which animal food predominates.
4. That it is the meal which, upon a necessity arising for the abolition of all *but* one, would naturally offer itself as the one.

The first and third elements were surely present, and perhaps the fourth also. Only the second was absent. Though the great dinners were going or gone, an invitation to dinner remained more flattering than an invitation to lunch. The menus might be barely distinguishable, the pomp was more marked, and in the hour or two of intercourse following dinner there was a measure of hospitality and regard which no luncheon could offer.

Confusion, too, was spreading with education. For some distance down the social scale men and women living just the same lives as the lawyers' clerks in Mrs. Henry Wood's novel, dining at one and eating a high tea at home in the evening, were genteelly defying De Quincey by christening their midday meal lunch, though there was no dinner to come and no one was deceived into supposing that there was.[1] Since their midday meal, whatever they called it, seldom compared for sustenance with the chops and steaks of those lawyers' clerks, the habit of a snack in the middle of the morning and afternoon tea half-way through the afternoon now became general in every office, making five or six daily deliveries of food, at three-hour intervals, to the stomach.

Returning once more up the social scale, we find the same tendency at the top. By the nineteen-thirties, the fashionable ladies of London were consuming breakfast, lunch, afternoon tea, the 'coloured wormcasts' of a cocktail buffet, dinner at 8.45 or 9, and supper in the small hours, in

[1] The dungaree worker, the plumber, or the house painter, knocking off for half an hour at 10 in the morning, still calls the snack his 'lunch'.

semi-darkness, and in snatches. For them, too, lunch was often the most, the only, considerable meal of a day which, with the possible omission of afternoon tea, was observed by their husbands and brothers. They might still occupy the family house, they might still, without knowing it, dance to Waldteufel. But to their grandparents, in fifty short years, it would all—the family life, the warm, scented house, the extraordinary drinks, the stained hearth, the old tunes with their rhythm violated and their melody masked—have become unrecognizable.

Though worse was to come, life between the wars was hectic, and it is hard not to conclude that people of almost every class were finding, in the multiplication of small meals, in the constant interruption of normal activities, a form of narcotic against the strain of existence. They resisted, while surrendering to, chain-smoking. They gave way, with something like inattention, to chain-eating. Compared with the Asiatic and even with the continental, the English stomach has always been a short runner, emitting signs of distress after four and a half hours and in loud rebellion at five. For the last twenty or twenty-five years now it has been widely excused from running altogether.

Nevertheless, in the blurred and spotted pattern which won favour in the days before the Second World War, the hours of breakfast, lunch, and tea underwent no marked, or no relative, change. Only dinner went on being pushed round the clock till it sometimes reached, as has been said, 9 o'clock, the most advanced time yet recorded. How much farther it would have gone, whether it could have gone any farther, are questions we cannot answer and which perhaps never will be answered. The ladies have changed direction, though not their disarming smile; their ambition is now aimed at the provision of meals designed less to please or even satisfy than to use as little crockery and cutlery as possible; and in their eyes the traveller refreshing himself at the station buffet, a saucerless cup in one hand, a plateless sandwich in the other, has succeeded the warrior, the gentleman, and the banker in the long series of ideal men.

The foregoing paragraph contains, as the reader has noted, a comment tremendous in its implications. In the 150 years leading to the day when Pope complained of being asked to wait till 4 o'clock for his dinner, the meal had moved approximately four hours round the clock; and when the young American in *Flickerbridge* exclaimed at the 'immense' hour of 8, another century and a half had gone by. On the one hand the rate of progress was remarkably steady, on the other it could not continue without bringing dinner eventually to midnight, and beyond. The meal did, as we have seen, struggle as far as 9, but even without the revolution of the past decade it must surely have been helpless to proceed. Yet that admission means that the day had reached stabilization-point—something which, in modern times, had never happened before, something which, indeed, could scarcely have endured. We do not have to look far to find causes at work which, even without the war, would have set dinner retracing its steps. There was 'the servant problem'; there was dinner's traditional restlessness and its inability, at last, to move in any direction save backwards. It may not go back step by step over the whole distance, for that would mean the surrender of the nineteenth century's great gift to mankind, the afternoon. But it might conceivably jump back to 1 o'clock; it might bestow its name, as it has already yielded much of its activity, to lunch, and be gazetted as supper. That seems at least, if no more than, a possibility. There are others—such as the disappearance of meals altogether into the unending snack, an undistinguishable population indistinguishably nibbling, rabbits in a national park. Already large sections of the public, absent-mindedly munching, must find it difficult to say at any given moment whether they are enjoying elevenses, lunch, tea, or some chance, additional makeshift. Their needs are reflected and met by countless small premises—not quite sweet-shops, not quite tea-shops, not altogether snack bars —where indeterminate refreshment is always available and meals never served. In such places kedgeree, for example— a whole haddock, garnished with rice, butter, and egg—is soothingly listed as an 'In-between', a stop-gap which does nothing to blunt relish of the impending meal, a knob to keep the fire from sinking.[1]

Great repasts demand a cheap and abundant supply of both food and domestics, and in the accessible parts of the globe these requirements can be found only among the barbarous, the semi-barbarous, or at least the backward nations. Great repasts are themselves, perhaps, barbaric; in Europe, as well as in North America, they seem to have passed into limbo, and nowhere have they slipped away more rapidly than in Great Britain. At present the wealthier

[1] In Frith's picture (1854) of holiday-makers at Ramsgate, there are over 100 figures, men, women, and children, and not one of them is absorbing refreshment. Could any beach-photographer today find anywhere a group equally large and equally abstemious?

grades of society, unable to offer suitable entertainment at home and addicted, no less than their fellows, to the easy path, invite their friends to catering establishments. Even this substitute is in danger. It is an open secret that some of the great clubs, inadequately staffed and likely to remain so, are contemplating the institution of cafeteria service; it may be a mere question of time before restaurants are driven to the same device.

All this—the day-long snacking, the flight of domestics, cafeteria service—comes from what is known as the rise in the standard of living. The day, like the nation, has undergone a simultaneous levelling-up and levelling-down, and now presents an appearance unbroken, unless by the ruminating jaw and the searching tongue. The alimentary prospect now, as in all ages, closely resembles the political, and in an unending meal of food from tins transferred to cellophane wrappings and eaten at no set times we should not be far from mob rule. It is useless to repine. Indeed, the arts of cooking and eating, of selecting bottles and guests, may prove a trifling price for the blessing of living in the twentieth century. One can never be sure of the future. Therein lies the attraction of the past.

But if the war which began in 1939 merely stimulated and made clear certain changes already latent, it originated others. Everyone who could do so, women as well as men, formed the habit of lunching at a restaurant or club or canteen, thereby eking out the rations, ensuring at least one fairly good meal a day, and discounting in advance the violent interruptions to which the evening was prone. In winter, especially, a husband who had failed to eat a sustaining lunch found himself greeted at home with no extravagant signs of affection. But since the restaurants, too, were rationed, clients soon learned that an early arrival, before the best dishes were exhausted, had advantages; they changed their lunch hour from 1 to 12.30, then to 12 or even 11.45. By the end of the war the majority of Londoners were eating as much as they could get at noon, having a light meal early in the evening, and indulging more and more their old fondness for odd morsels at odd times.

When the war ended, the continuation of rationing preserved the supremacy, and the displacement, of lunch; limitations of public transport and domestic help took over the work of the bombers in discouraging entertainment of friends at night. In time, after a year or two, food grew a little more plentiful, trains and buses ran a little later, but by then the population was subject to a ten-year-old habit as difficult to break as that other habit imposed by war-time restrictions, the ordering of three courses, never more and never less, from a bill of fare. Liberation, besides being fitful, does not always meet with appreciation; on the whole the public has not favoured attempts to restore the 8.30 theatre, though it has consented to a change from 7 o'clock to 7.30. To have something to eat after the play is now a good deal easier than it was; it is also a little easier to eat beforehand. While these pages were being written, I have seen a notice from a small restaurant announcing that dinner is obtainable at 5.30, and another, from a smarter establishment, offering a meal at 5.45. There were people in the first decade of the nineteenth century who would have regarded such hours as slightly bourgeois.

Dinner will possibly recover some of, it can hardly get back all, it might continue to lose, its prestige. The ladies, no doubt, will decide and, unlike their mothers with their 9 o'clocks, they have plenty of elbow room. But they are not their mothers, theirs is not the world their mothers knew, and their estimate of what might be smart is coloured by their experience of what is worth while.

Leaving the unpredictable future to develop along its own lines, as well as to decide whether what we now call lunch should be called dinner and what we call dinner given the name of supper, or whether indeed De Quincey is worth bothering about at all, we might do worse than look back on our journey, consulting once again the daily programmes of young Miss Holroyd (p. 17) and François de la Roche-foucauld (p. 22). Half-way through the intervening years came a long period during which England attained a prosperity greater than ever before or since. That prosperity was purchased by hard work. The labouring classes had the hardest work, the worst conditions, and the greatest suffer-ings, the upper and middle classes paying their supplement in the shape of leisure. Whatever one may think of it, a bargain was struck, there was a *quid pro quo*. But we today, having no longer that prosperity, cannot help noticing that neither have we the leisure with which it was bought. We have only the hard work, the shortage of time, the inappro-priate habits of another age. We are much to be pitied, and we often say so.

Widely differing, yet all cushioned and comfortable in the middle ranks of society, the people whose fortunes we have been following inherited and maintained a tradition of living—a living tradition capable of growth and change and, as we are now brought to see, of sickness and decrepitude. For its health, it depended on the services, seldom appreciated and often abused, of a domestic staff which has fled. Lacking those services, the tradition itself, so sure, so strong, so apparently indestructible, is on the danger list. If we like to anticipate its demise, to discover its successor, we must presumably look across the world and into the future, sweep the horizons of space and time. Nothing of that sort will happen here, it is outside the scope of a discussion which can now be adjourned for a generation or two.